D1626585

The Little Book
of
CHINESE
PROVERBS

Dedicated to
Simon & Dani

The Little Book

of

CHINESE

PROVERBS

~

Compiled by

JONATHAN CLEMENTS

SIENA

This edition published and distributed by Siena, 1999

Siena is an imprint of Parragon

Parragon
Queen Street House
4 Queen Street
Bath BA1 1HE

Produced by Magpie Books, an imprint of
Robinson Publishing Ltd, London

Copyright © Parragon 1999

All rights reserved. This book is sold subject to the condition
that it shall not, by way of trade or otherwise, be lent, re-sold,
hired out or otherwise circulated in any form of binding or cover
other than that in which it is published and without a similar
condition including this condition being imposed on the
subsequent purchaser.

ISBN 0 75252 769 X

A copy of the British Library Cataloguing-in-Publication Data
is available from the British Library
Printed in China

Contents

꿔

Introduction

𝕏

The English-speaking world is often too wrapped up in itself to notice other cultures. Even in the wider, Western world, the mysteries of the Far East remain mysterious partly because so few mainstream works are prepared to tackle them. As this book will show, the concerns of the Chinese people are much like those of any other. They laugh, they cry, they tell jokes and they get into squabbles. Over the centuries, they have also provided us with many phrases that we now take for granted. There was a time when nobody had heard that the grass was greener on the other side, when no one scoffed at the thought of a paper tiger, and when none had heard that many a true word is spoken in jest. And yet we share many of these ideas with the Chinese, either through coincidence or a long-forgotten meeting of cultures. This book gives approximate dates where available for many of these sayings so the reader can see just how old they are.

When even the large dictionaries of quotations struggle to contain a few dozen Chinese proverbs, a little book like this can hardly redress the balance. Where known, attributions have been given, but the Chinese practice of alluding to classical books means that many wise men are in fact quoting the words of even older sages. This practice continues today; though Deng Xiaoping famously said: "What matter if a cat is black or white, so long as it catches mice," he was not coining a phrase, but repeating an age-old saying. Many famous quotations from Chinese history actually begin with the words "We all know the phrase . . ." or "As the ancients used to say . . ." showing that these proverbs have an even older provenance. For this reason, perhaps a fifth of the quotes in this book are simply filed as "Traditional." Even in modern times, many writers are unwilling to be identified for fear of persecution, which has occasioned several cases in the book of an anonymous saying attached to a definite date.

Particularly large numbers of proverbs are clustered in a brief era about 2500 years ago, at the end of the Zhou Dynasty. This is chiefly because this was the time at which the great sages of Chinese history lived: Lao Zi, Confucius (Kong Qiu), Mencius (Meng Zi) and their followers. It became customary for the Chinese to allude to the masters, and for over two thousand years, one was only considered educated if one could regurgitate the words of the Classics verbatim. This has meant that most of the Chinese proverbs known in the West, and, indeed, the majority of those contained within this book, are the sayings of a handful of men. To imply otherwise would be misleading.

A proverb in China can be many things. This book collects a number of wise sayings, but also many quotes from songs and famous poems, which are often used proverbially in Chinese conversation. The Book of Songs collects hundreds of ancient poems, almost all anonymous. The Imperial Yue-fu (or Music Bureau) kept records of the most popular songs in order to show the Emperor the general mood of the country. In this way, the Yue-fu songs are as accurate a barometer of public feeling as the modern pop charts, and many of the songs are truly timeless. Just as today, many phrases from the lyrics worked their way into conversations and became proverbial in their own right. Similarly, a Chinese proverb can come from an anonymous piece of folklore, often based on a chance pun or a long-forgotten past event. Some of these have been included, too – readers may have seen them before in the occasional fortune cookie.

Readers should be aware that this book employs the Pinyin romanization system for ease of pronunciation, and that many familiar quotations may be listed under unfamiliar names. Beijing has always been pronounced "Beijing," but under the antiquated Wade-Giles system it is written "Peking" even though it is pronounced "Beijing." Those searching in this book for Sun Tzu, the author of the famous Art of War, *will need to look for Sun Zi; those looking for the philosopher Chuang Tzu should instead search out Zhuang Zi; and those wishing to find sayings of Mao Tse-tung should instead search for Mao Zedong.*

Table of Chinese Dynasties

Xia Dynasty	2100–1600 BC
Shang Dynasty	1600–1100 BC
Zhou Dynasty	1100–221 BC
(Spring and Autumn Period)	770–476 BC
(Warring States Period)	475–221 BC
Qin Dynasty	221–207 BC
Han Dynasty	206 BC–220 AD
Three Kingdoms Period	220–280
Jin Dynasty	265–420
Southern and Northern Dynasties*	420–589
Sui Dynasty	581–618
Tang Dynasty	618–907

*(Southern and Northern Dynasties include Song, Qi, Liang, Chen, North, East & West Wei, North Qi and Northern Zhou)

Five Dynasties and Ten Kingdoms	907–979
Song (North and South)	960–1279
Liao	916–1125
Kin	1115–1234
Yuan	1271–1368
Ming	1368–1644
Qing	1644–1912
Republic	1912–1949
People's Republic	1949–Present Day

Chapter 1

#

WAR & POLITICS

The first historical Emperor, in 221 BC, was Qin Shi Huang-di, mainly known today for the army of Terracotta Warriors that guards his grave. In his time he was a successful but tyrannical ruler, who burned most of the books then in existence in order to stifle debate. The Chinese Classics we have today, including Confucius and the Book of Changes, are among the few survivors of this dark moment in Chinese history.

And yet this was also the period that created China itself. Ever since the time of the Qin Emperor, China has struggled to remain a single entity; a single dynasty would hold the country together for a time, but then the country would be thrown once more into internal turmoil. The Three Kingdoms and the period known as the Southern and Northern Dynasties, for example, were times when

China possessed no single ruler. And twice, "Chinese" dynasties were nothing of the sort: the Yuan was a period of Mongol rule and during the Qing the Chinese were ruled by the foreign Manchu.

From the time of the Qin Emperor, however, unity was always the ultimate goal, and Chinese philosophers coined pithy words about politics and warfare. For many, war and politics were inextricably linked, a fact Chairman Mao well understood when he said: "Political power grows out of the barrel of a gun." Confucius occupied himself with rule by example, attempting to encourage political harmony by encouraging individual friendship. However, legalists like Han Fei Zi claimed that only lies and threats could keep the population in line. The tension between these two schools has remained, as genteel souls raised during peacetime find themselves unable to stomach the injustices of war, and martial types forced to come home after a campaign find themselves unable to bear the traditions and rules of a peaceful court. War is never welcomed, but seen as a sign of failure; if there is unrest, it is because Heaven is angry. If Heaven is angry, it is because the people of Earth have failed to do their duty.

To defeat an army, you must capture the leader.

Du Fu, Tang Dynasty

⁂

If the chariot ahead has overturned, let the chariot behind beware.

Jia Yi, Han Dynasty

⁂

It is better to be broken jade than a rude, whole clay pot.
(Death before dishonor)

Yuan Jinghao, Zhou Dynasty

⁂

Seek peace at the city walls.
(Bargain when you – and your army – have the advantage)

Traditional

Better for one family to weep than a hundred clans.
(The needs of the many outweigh the needs of the few)

Fan Zhongyan, Song Dynasty

Whosoever breaks this treaty will dishonor our ancestors. Hence the people of Lu fear nothing.

Zhan Xi to the invading Duke Xiao,
Spring and Autumn Period

Just a few more arrows, and we could fight again. But our arrows are gone and our swords and spears are broken. Lest we be captured at daybreak, let us flee under the cover of night like birds and beasts.

General Li Ling to his outnumbered soldiers,
Western Han Dynasty

When a deer's life is in danger, it will seek sanctuary where it can.

> *Duke Ling is warned that his invasion of a*
> *small state will unite his enemies against him,*
> *Spring and Autumn Period*

I announce to you these three laws.
1: Murders shall be executed.
2: Those who injure others shall pay the penalty.
3: Thieves shall be punished.

> *Liu Bang lays down the law to his victorious army,*
> *Han Dynasty*

A real man dies on a battlefield, and his body is wrapped in horsehide. Who wants to die in bed, surrounded by his wife and children?

General Ma Yuan chooses to die with his boots on,
Eastern Han Dynasty

Ruling the country is not difficult, it is just like herding horses. If a horse gives you trouble, take it out of the herd.

A boy wrangler makes it all seem easy to
the Yellow Emperor, c. 3000 BC

A prince must deal with unrest as a peasant deals with weeds. He must dig it up by the roots, so that it will not grow again.

Zhou Ren, Zhou Dynasty

An arrogant and complacent leader is sure to meet with defeat.

Dou Bobi, Tang Dynasty

When the birds are dead, the bow is put away. When the rabbit is dead, the hunting-dog is next on the menu. When the enemy is defeated, the allies should look to themselves.

The mercenary Fan Li warns Wen Zhong to get out while he can, Spring and Autumn Period

An arrow at the end of its journey is weak, so that it cannot even pierce thin silk.

Han Anguo advises negotiation instead of an
exhausting battle, Han Dynasty

My country has an old tradition, we send great men as envoys to great kings, and idiots as envoys to incompetent kings. Because I am the worst of all, they sent me to see you.

Ambassador Yan Ying kindly explains his
appointment to the sharp-tongued Duke Ling,
Spring and Autumn Period

To gain the respect of the people, several victories would not go amiss.

Shi Hou advises the usurper Zhou Yu,
Spring and Autumn Period

It is foolish to anger the majority, nor is it wise to do simply as you please. If your deeds displease the people, then disaster will surely follow.

Zi Chan talks Zi Kong around during a labor dispute,
Spring and Autumn Period

The jackals and wolves run riot. There is no time for sorrow and mourning. Turn to the matter in hand, otherwise you shall open the gate and welcome in a thief.

Zhang Zhao exhorts Sun Quan to do what has to be done,
Eastern Han Dynasty

If we attack now the enemy will split like a bamboo stem. After the initial cut, the blade flies easily.

Du Yu predicts that his men will advance like a knife through butter (or bamboo), Western Jin Dynasty

Decisions should not be too clear. Otherwise, when things go wrong you will have to take the blame. Keep it vague.

Su Weidao on the secrets of management, Tang Dynasty

If anyone wants courage, come here and buy some! I still have so much courage left over, I can sell the surplus on!

Gao Gu modestly encourages others to come and have a go if they think they're hard enough, Spring and Autumn Period

When riding a tiger, it is difficult to get off. The only way may be to kill it.

Wen Qiao advises that there is no turning back,
Eastern Jin Dynasty

❀

When the men first hear the beat of the war-drums, their courage is greatest. With the second drum, their ardor starts to fade, and by the third, it has all but faded away.

Cao Gui advises against expending effort too early,
Spring and Autumn Period

❀

I've heard that he who strikes first can defeat the enemy. He who strikes last will be beaten.

Rebel general Xiang Liang, Qin Dynasty

With men as with silk, it is most difficult to change colors once the dye has set.

Mo Zi, Warring States Period

A tyrannical goverment is worse than a man-eating tiger.

Confucius, Spring and Autumn Period

I never give my tigers live prey, lest their ardor be aroused for the hunt. Nor do I feed them whole carcasses, lest their interest quicken for tearing flesh. The tiger and man are quite alike, in that he is fond of those who feed him and give him succor. He kills only when provoked.

Liang Yang, Imperial zoo-keeper and tiger-tamer,
Zhou Dynasty

One does not need a lantern when the sun or moon is shining. Watering cans are not required when the garden has rain. Thanks to you, the empire prospers. There is no reason for me to stay on the throne; take it from me.

The legendary Emperor Yao offers his crown to minister Xu Yu, c. 2300 BC

A bird may rest on a branch in the forest. A thirsty rat may sip from a stream. I have no more need than these insignificant creatures.

Xu Yu graciously declines the Emperor's offer, c. 2300 BC

In good times, the wise man works for the state. In bad times, he looks after himself.

Jie Yu, Spring and Autumn Period

The common people secure their chests and money-bags with ropes, lest a thief break in and steal them. They consider this to be a wise precaution. Then a thief enters, who carries off the locked and bound treasure, giving thanks that someone has wrapped his bounty for him. Statecraft and governorship are the same: those who the mass of the people call wise are nothing but wrappers for thieves.

Zhuang Zi, Warring States Period

Laws and customs must vary in accordance with the times. What will happen if you dress a monkey in the manner of the Duke of Zhou? He will rend it with his teeth and claws, and only be satisfied when the costume is fully torn away. Times past and the present day are as different as the Duke of Zhou and a monkey. Do not dress modern people in the garments of their ancestors; do not follow ancient ways for the sake of it.

Jin the Musician, Spring and Autumn Period

❧

A minister should serve his lord with honor. Or he should resign.

Confucius, Spring and Autumn Period

❧

Emperor Yu corrupted the soul of mankind by legalizing murder. He claimed that in war, one killed enemies, not men, and that this was not evil.

Lao Zi, Spring and Autumn Period

Opportunity must not be lost while the gods smile.
Li Jing, Tang Dynasty

✵

In order to live a long time, one must not contend with others, but think and do as everyone else.
Zhuang Zi, Warring States Period

✵

Take care of the small things.
Xun Zi, Warring States Period

✵

When away we marched
The weeping willow hung with green
Now I return through mists and sleet, rain and sleet
Hungry, thirsty, with weeping in my heart
None can know my sorrow
A soldier's return, "Picking Ferns,"
Book of Songs, Zhou Dynasty

Shrimp may attack dragons in shallow water.

Traditional

⁂

The cat does not weep for the rat.

Traditional

⁂

A war wastes the people, the enemy and the leader, who is eaten up with anxiety.

Xu Wugui, Warring States Period

⁂

The violent man shall die a violent death.

Lao Zi, Spring and Autumn Period

All the crops are rotting raw
All the days we march to order
All the men are sent to war
Guard we must the country's border
All the grasses black become
All the soldiers with disease
How was our good will undone?
What has made us us ill at ease?
On the plains no tigers found
Oxen too have fled from sight
Saddened soldiers hold their ground
Resting not, through day and night
Through the bushes foxes run
Tails and shadows in the grasses
To the battle soldiers come
Chariot after chariot passes

"All the Grasses Turning Yellow,"
Book of Songs, Zhou Dynasty

飛

People are obedient to the ruler who promotes the righteous and condemns the evil.

Confucius, Spring and Autumn Period

Pioneers plant trees, but the latecomers rest in the shade.

Traditional

Sending untrained recruits into battle is sending them to their graves.

Confucius, Spring and Autumn Period

The straightest tree is the first to be cut down.
The well with the sweetest water is the first to be drained.

Duke Ren, Spring and Autumn Period

I look about me but see hope
A forlorn wish to return
The birds may fly south
The fox may die in his den
But I am exiled through no fault of my own
A forlorn wish to return
That must be forgotten

Chu Yuan, Warring States Period

☽

Fighting south of the ramparts
Death north of the wall
In the wilderness, bodies left as food for the birds
I beg the crows: "Show some respect
For these men left unburied
Spare their rotting flesh"

Yue-fu: Nineteen Ancient Poems, Han Dynasty

☽

Where are my brave warriors, to guard my four
frontiers?

Liu Bang, Han Dynasty

No rice in the larder, no clothes in the chamber
So he buckles on his sword and marches for the East
  Gate
The mother of his children pulling, weeping at his
  sleeve, saying:
"Others dream of wealth and glory, their eyes on the
  blue sky above
But look you to the face of your son
Let us stay poor but stay together! Don't go!"
But he says: "I have no choice! Away! I'm already late!
Already my hair turns white, no one lives forever."
                Yue-fu: Nineteen Ancient Poems, Han Dynasty

Poke the flames and burn yourself.

                                        Traditional

Heroes are made by the times.

                                        Traditional

A state that is great carries the seeds of its demise, just as a giant tree singles itself out for the blow of the axe. Weakness brings life, strength brings death.

Lao Zi, Spring and Autumn Period

A wise ruler must suppress his personal hatreds.

Bao Shu Ya, Zhou Dynasty

Rivers flood for a mere three days, storms blow over in a matter of hours. My family is at the height of its powers. Perhaps it shall fall.

The victorious Zhao Xiang Zi refuses to look on the bright side, Spring and Autumn Period

At the border many strong men
Back at home, many widows.

Chen Lin, Eastern Han Dynasty

At fifteen years I went to war, coming home at eighty

I saw someone from my village and said: "Anyone at
home?"

But he said: "There's your home, all overgrown

With trees and gravestones left untended

Wild rabbits in the kennel, and pheasants on the
rafters

Wild rice grows in the courtyard, and mallows in the
well

You could grind the grains for rice and use the
mallow for soup."

"But for whom?" I replied, walking through the East
Gate

My tears falling till my clothes were drenched.

Yue-fu: Nineteen Ancient Poems, Han Dynasty

Bears hunt me in pairs; tigers and leopards growl
    along the road
The valley is almost deserted, I squint through the
    thick snow
But see no end in sight. And still I have far to go
My heart wells with great sadness
If only I could return to the East

Cao Cao, Eastern Han Dynasty

Look beneath the Great Wall, and you will see bones
upon bones of dead men.

Chen Lin, Eastern Han Dynasty

He climbed the distant hills in search of fame
But now lies dead beneath the Tartar's hooves
He hardly saw the wife who bore his name
Such is the lot of men, hard life, few loves
Bao Zhao, Northern Wei Dynasty

A general's triumph means ten thousand rotting bones.

Traditional

The other courtiers think of you as a mountain. I think of you as a mountain of ice.
Zhang Tuan refuses to flatter Emperor Xuanzong,
Tang Dynasty

Do not steal the words of others, nor repeat them as an echo does the thunder.

Book of Rites, Zhou Dynasty

Though brothers may have private feud
They fight as one against the alien foe.
Book of Songs, Zhou Dynasty

I recommend good men for the country's sake, and
not for my own purposes.
Di Renzhi, Tang Dynasty

Although I am thin in appearance, the Empire is fat.
Emperor Xuanzong, Tang Dynasty

My wish is that the royal heart may turn into brilliant
light, not to illuminate the banquets of the rich, but
the deserted homes of the fugitive people.
Nie Yizhong, Tang Dynasty

You have a heart of stone and bowels of iron.
Pi Rixiu to Song Qing, Tang Dynasty

✺

His mouth still smells of mother's milk.
Liu Bang thinks little of Bo Zhi, Han Dynasty

✺

To give peace to the Empire and suppress rebellion, a large sword and a long spear are necessary. What use is a pen?
Shi Hungzhao, Five Dynasties and Ten Kingdoms

✺

Is a knife of lead not sharp enough for one cut?
Min Wangcheng just wants one chance, Jin Dynasty

✺

The views of men of wise counsel are much the same.
Liu Bei, Three Kingdoms

The beauty of the fir and pine is enhanced by winter snows, while is it the nature of the rush and willow to fade at the first breath of autumn.

Gu Yuezhi explains why he has gone prematurely gray,
Eastern Jin Dynasty

❀

Ten men cannot defeat a thousand tigers.

Chang Anmin, Song Dynasty

❀

Be stern with the smaller states. It will be as easy as setting a dog to catch a limping hare.

Fan Zhu, Warring States Period

❀

In courage desire greatness and in thought desire carefulness.

Liu Su, Tang Dynasty

It is harder to deal with the weeds once they have spread.

Traditional

Building a house by the roadside takes more than three years.

Zhang Di warns that public actions attract public attention, Han Dynasty

The wrath of the mob is difficult to oppose. The desire of the individual is difficult to accomplish.

Zuo Qiuming, Spring and Autumn Period

The secret of leading soldiers is having a single leader.

Yue Wumu warns that too many cooks can spoil the broth, Song Dynasty

Emperor Wu of the Han Dynasty was inwardly a man of many passions, though outwardly he made a show of kindness and honor.

Wen Zhuang, Ming Dynasty

True gold fears not the test of fire.

Traditional

War is like a fire; if you do not put aside your weapons, they will eventually consume you.

Li Chuan, Tang Dynasty

There is no victory in winning a hundred battles. There is victory in subduing your enemy without fighting at all.

Sun Zi, Spring and Autumn Period

❀

The art of war lies in thwarting the enemy's plans, in breaking up his alliances, and then, only then, in attacking his army.

Sun Zi, Spring and Autumn Period

❀

He is victorious who knows when and when not to fight.

Sun Zi, Spring and Autumn Period

❀

Five qualities are dangerous in a leader. If reckless, he can be killed. If cowardly, he can be captured. If impulsive, he can be tricked. If proud, he can be humiliated. If kind, he can be tormented.

Sun Zi, Spring and Autumn Period

He who governs by example is like the Pole Star, which keeps its place while the other stars turn around it.

Confucius, Spring and Autumn Period

He who is moved neither by slander that gradually seeps into the mind, nor by statements that startle like a wound in the flesh, can be called intelligent indeed.

Confucius, Spring and Autumn Period

Good government is attained when those who are near are made happy, and those who are far away are attracted.

Confucius, Spring and Autumn Period

Heaven and Earth are not humane, they regard all things as straw dogs.
(i.e. as disposable tokens for sacrifice)

Lao Zi, Spring and Autumn Period

❀

All men strive to grasp what they do not know, while none strive to grasp what they already know; and all strive to discredit those things in which they do not excel. This is why there is chaos,

Zhuang Zi, Warring States Period

❀

When the first indications of error begin to appear in the state, Heaven sends forth ominous portents and calamities to warn men and announce the fact.

Dong Zhongshu, Han Dynasty

Armament is an important factor in war, but not the decisive factor. Man, not material, forms the decisive factor.

Mao Zedong, *People's Republic*

Let a hundred flowers bloom, and let a hundred schools of thought contend.

Mao Zedong, *People's Republic*

Other men are the carving knife and serving dish; we are the fish and the meat.

Sun Yat-sen, *Republic*

The life of our people will be elevated if we live artistically; we will become wealthy if we live productively and we will be safe if we lead a military way of life.

Chiang Kai-shek, Republic

We should support whatever the enemy opposes and oppose whatever the enemy supports.

Mao Zedong, People's Republic

When the enemy asks for a truce without warning, he is up to something.

Sun Zi, Spring and Autumn Period

A leader's troops may join him in rejoicing at the accomplishment, but not in laying the plans.

Cao Cao, Han Dynasty

I scratch my white head, and the hair is yet thinner.

Du Fu, Tang Dynasty

※

In the wilderness, there is weeping,
When a thousand homes hear the approach of war.

Du Fu, Tang Dynasty

※

Malicious warring of barbarians brings the Emperor's great anger.

Li Bo, Tang Dynasty

※

Border guards are food for the wolves and tigers.

Li Bo, Tang Dynasty

※

Today's men are not those of yesterday.

Li Bo, Tang Dynasty

Since ancient times, a great achievement has always ended with a greater failure.

Li Bo, Tang Dynasty

✿

Having a son is unlucky indeed.
These days it is better to have a daughter.
Your daughter can be married to your neighbor
Your son will be buried under the weeds.

Du Fu warns of the winds of war, Tang Dynasty

✿

My brother went to war, my aunt died.
Dusk went, morning came. Colors changed.

Bo Juyi records a female musician's lament,
Tang Dynasty

✿

The swing of a sword cannot cut the mist from the sky.

Li He, Tang Dynasty

Kingdoms rise and kingdoms fall, but it's the common people who suffer.

Zhang Yanghao, Yuan Dynasty

❈

When the work of the perfect leader is done well, the people think they have done it all by themselves.

Lao Zi, Spring and Autumn Period

❈

When the hot water for the bath is ready, the lice commiserate among themselves.

The Huai Nan Zi, Han Dynasty

❈

Sorrow, sorrow like rain.

Li Bo, Tang Dynasty

These so called "arms" are really the tools of murderers.

Li Bo, Tang Dynasty

✥

The strongest women till the fields,
Yet crops come not as before.

Du Fu, Tang Dynasty

✥

The Emperor travels this way. Joy without end!
Su Ting composes a poem for the Emperor (funnily enough), Tang Dynasty

✥

Men always march to war. But how many return home?

Wang Han, Tang Dynasty

Through the night, soldiers turn their eyes towards home.

Li Yi, Tang Dynasty

🦋

One must consider most carefully, before frowning or laughing.

Traditional

🦋

He that has committed no crime by day, fears not a knock on the door by night.

Traditional

🦋

Good and evil both end up in the grave, but a jest may bring about an untimely death.

Traditional

Keep your mouth shut when required.

Traditional

✿

Refrain from exalting the worthy, so that people will not scheme and contend. Refrain from prizing rare possessions, so that people will not steal. Refrain from displaying objects of desire, so that people's hearts will not be disturbed.

Lao Zi, Spring and Autumn Period

✿

It was when the country fell into chaos and confusion that there was talk of loyalty and trust.

Lao Zi, Spring and Autumn Period

✿

The foundation of the world lies in the nation, the foundation of the nation lies in the family, and the foundation of the family lies in the individual.

Mencius, Warring States Period

Men must be keen in matters of government, as the earth is keen on making things grow.

Confucius (attrib.), Spring and Autumn Period

❀

The administration of government depends on the right men.

Zi Si, Warring States Period

❀

Claiming certainty without corroborating evidence is stupid.

Han Fei Zi, Warring States Period

❀

Now the sovereign would tax the rich and give to the poor. This amounts to robbing the diligent and the frugal and rewarding the extravagant and the lazy.

Han Fei Zi, Warring States Period

It would be impossible to expect the people to fight hard against the enemy but to refrain from private feuds.

Han Fei Zi, Warring States Period

When the wise man becomes a ruler, he does not expect the people to do good themselves, but takes steps to ensure that they are prevented from doing evil.

Han Fei Zi, Warring States Period

Government is not for one man.

Han Fei Zi, Warring States Period

※

Only those who are ignorant about government insist
on winning the hearts of the people.

Han Fei Zi, Warring States Period

※

The intelligence of the masses is not to be respected
or relied upon.

Han Fei Zi, Warring States Period

※

The ruler should show no favor and grant no pardon.

Han Fei Zi, Warring States Period

All crimes should be punished, and yet knights are feted for their readiness to draw their swords.

Han Fei Zi, Warring States Period

҉

Subtle and mysterious theories are no business of the common people.

Han Fei Zi, Warring States Period

҉

The wise ruler uses a man's skills, but does not listen to his suggestions.

Han Fei Zi, Warring States Period

҉

Kings and nobles, generals and ministers: such men are made, not born.

Chen She, Qin Dynasty

Loving all creatures [the ideal ruler] does not reward in joy or punish in anger, and thereby he may be benevolent.

Dong Zhongshu, Han Dynasty

If the institutions of former kings are not suitable, they should be abolished.

The Huai Nan Zi, Han Dynasty

There is one fundamental principle in statecraft, and that is to consider the well-being of the people as fundamental.

The Huai Nan Zi, Han Dynasty

Why must there be any immutable laws?

The Huai Nan Zi, Han Dynasty

Feed the soldiers for a thousand days. Use them for one.

Traditional

※

Man in society cannot get away from his fellow beings.

Guo Xiang, Han Dynasty

※

Only those who have no minds of their own and do not use their own judgment can adapt themselves to changes and not be burdened by them.

Guo Xiang, Han Dynasty

Patience is a tree with bitter roots that bears sweet
fruits.

Traditional

When a thousand people gather together with no one
as their leader, they will be either unruly or
disorganized. Therefore when there are many
virtuous people, there should not be many rulers, but
when there is no virtuous person, there should be a
ruler.

Guo Xiang, Han Dynasty

It was my intention to fight to a finish, desisting only
when all my ships were sunk and all my men dead.
But I cannot bring myself to cause the death of
thousands more.

Admiral Ding Ruchang to Admiral Ito,
Qing Dynasty

Great generals need not blow their own trumpets.

Traditional

※

Though on a throne, I'm moved by other thoughts
Unknown to courtiers who attend to me.

Emperor Wen Cong, Tang Dynasty

※

A sacred peach that waxes green with heaven's dew,
An apricot favored by sun and clouds are you.
But I, hibiscus, by a stream, for autumn wait,
Nor blame the tardy east wind that I blossom late.

Gao Chan is just a late bloomer, Tang Dynasty

※

My strength plucked up the hills,
My might shadowed the world;
But the times were against me.

Xiang Yu, Han Dynasty

Nothing brings greater misfortune than killing those who have already surrendered.

Wang Suo, Han Dynasty

To strive with all one's might for benevolence and righteousness, fearful always lest one fail to educate the people, this is the ambition of a statesman. To strive with all one's might for good and profit, fearful always of poverty and want, this is the business of ordinary people.

Dong Zhongshu, Han Dynasty

Catch not lice on a tiger's head.

Traditional

Some things even thunder cannot move.

Traditional

Once struggle is grasped, miracles are possible.

Mao Zedong, People's Republic

※

He who strikes first admits that his ideas have given out.

Traditional

※

If my prediction proves to be wrong, it will be a blessing to the state.

Su the Historian, Spring and Autumn Period

※

I have never heard of a finger being greater than an arm, nor of an arm being greater than a leg, but if such should exist, it could only indicate a serious disease!

Ying Hou, Warring States Period

When the fruit is heavy, the bough is strained, when the bough is strained, the trunk is harmed; when a capital is great it endangers the state, when a minister is strong he menaces his king.

Ying Hou, Warring States Period

"Among the dead", said the skull, "none is king, none is subject. There is no division of the seasons: for us the whole world is spring, the whole world is autumn. No monarch on his throne has joy greater than ours."

Zhuang Zi, Warring States Period

To win the battle, retain the surprise.

Traditional

Large chickens don't eat small rice.

Traditional

A big man can afford to bend and stretch.
Traditional

Pay out a long line to catch a big fish.
Traditional

If we can no longer speak of loyalty to princes, can we not, however, speak of loyalty to our people?
Sun Yat-sen, Qing Dynasty/Republican Period

Chapter 2

ЖЄ

HONOR & FRIENDSHIP

Emperors ruled by the "Mandate of Heaven." If Heaven became angry, the Emperor's powers to bring crops and rain would fail, and the people would revolt. Such revolts brought new dynasties to power, right up until the twentieth century, when the Emperor was finally deposed. The Emperor's job was to protect the country from harm by obeying the will of Heaven. Beneath the Emperor, mere mortals need only know their place and do their duty to keep things running smoothly. Honor and Friendship were important components of that duty.

From even before the time of Confucius, Chinese people were encouraged to live a virtuous life. One was indebted to one's family, and obliged to obey parents and care for younger family members. The Chinese definition of "family" stretched much further than the modern nuclear ideal; it included fifth and sixth cousins and great uncles once removed, all of whom were to be included in an honorable family's ceremonies.

Filial duty was of paramount importance; an Emperor once put a son to death for betraying his father, even when the father had committed a crime. Meanwhile, within the court the men were taught virtue but practiced politics. This chapter includes several examples of the flowery traditional greetings and overblown expressions which people were obliged to use in order to show that they understood their place in the honor system. A friend in need was truly a friend in deed when the whims of the Emperor and his ministers could change so fast and a chance comment could lead to death, exile or mutilation. Many of the great thinkers of Chinese history ended as the victims of court politics; Sun Zi with his feet cut off and Sima Qian blinded by imperial caprice. Ironic, then, that their failure in the court was what made them turn to writing. The deeds of those who wronged them are largely forgotten, and it is the words of the great thinkers that live on.

The Eight Confucian Virtues: Benevolence, Righteousness, Courtesy, Wisdom, Fidelity, Loyalty, Filial Piety and Service to Elders

Traditional

Beware a dagger hidden in a smile.

Shi Nai'an, Ming Dynasty

Check your wicked and sift out your vicious people before they come to China.

Lin Zexu to Queen Victoria, Qing Dynasty

Share joy and sorrow alike.

Duke Shanxiang, Zhou Dynasty

Gossip flies and spreads far.

Traditional

Better a fox's fur than the skins of a thousand sheep.
(To favor wise counsel over yes-men)

Zhao Yang, Spring and Autumn Period

Half a truth engenders a new lie.

Traditional

An old horse at the trough, still thinks of traveling a thousand leagues. A hero in his old age, never lets go of his principles.

Cao Cao, Eastern Han Dynasty

In death and life your friends are revealed, for richer for poorer, from riches to rags.

Lord Zhai notes that a friend in need is a friend in deed,
Western Han Dynasty

※

The Prince of Xiao acts with honor and speaks to us from the heart. We would wade through boiling water and walk on fire for him.

New recruits speak highly of their general,
Western Han Dynasty

※

Reputation is like a cake drawn on the ground. If you're hungry, it's not much help.

Emperor Ming explains that he is impressed by Lu Yu's
ability, not his resumé, Three Kingdoms Period

Hurting others will hurt oneself.

Traditional

❦

Although this bird has not yet taken flight, when it does it shall surpass heaven. Although it has not yet sung, when it does it shall shake the angels.

King Weiwang explains that he is biding his time,
Warring States Period

❦

From ancient times, men have mourned
Great things put to petty uses.

Lu You, Southern Song Dynasty

Suppose a soldier retreats fifty paces and mocks one who has retreated a hundred paces. Is this just or not?

Mencius warns King Huiwang against the pot calling the kettle black, Warring States Period

Often give, often receive.

Traditional

How can the swallow understand the aspirations of the swan?

Chen She, Qin Dynasty

Kong Yu was always prepared to listen and learn. He was not ashamed to consult his subjects, and even sought the advice of lesser men. Hence, when he died, he was called "The Learned One."

Confucius, Spring and Autumn Period

High-class songs find few singers. How can the average man comprehend my motives?

Song Yu, Warring States Period

He who commits too many sins marches on the road to death.

Duke Zhuanggong, Spring and Autumn Period

It is wrong not to repay the kindnesses of others, and to rejoice in their misfortunes.

Qing Zheng, Spring and Autumn Period

Only a storm truly tests the hardiness of a blade of grass.

Liu Xiu calls for a friend in need, Eastern Han Dynasty

❀

A clear conscience is the greatest armor.

Traditional

❀

Do not claim to be the disciple of a great teacher, lest your failures shame him.

Hu Zi, Eastern Zhou Dynasty

❀

The truly wise man does not display his wisdom. Such is the secret of being well-liked.

Yang Zhu, Zhou Dynasty

Those who seek fame, will only find it by extraordinary means. If you do only ordinary things, you will not even be famous within your own family. But that is preferable, in my opinion.

Shang Qiu Zi, Zhou Dynasty

Reputation should be neither sought nor avoided.

Lao Zi, Spring and Autumn Period

Suppress your desire for glory, and you will never be disappointed.

Emperor Yu, Xia Dynasty

Watch your words and your deeds, for your words shall be spoken and your deeds shall be copied.

Traditional

Good deeds attract glory, glory attracts fortune and fortune attracts enemies. Thus the wise man must think hard before doing a good deed.

Yang Zhu, Zhou Dynasty

✳

The wise man does not seek to influence the superficial. Instead, he sets an example of justice, which the just will follow.

Jie Yu, Spring and Autumn Period

✳

Is it not wonderful to put one's learning into practice? Is it not wonderful to welcome friends from afar? Is it not a gentleman who will not be offended if others fail to notice his great qualities?

Confucius subtly offers his services,
Spring and Autumn Period

When good is in danger, only a coward would not
defend it.

Confucius, Spring and Autumn Period

One who sets his heart on doing good, will ever be
free from evil.

Confucius, Spring and Autumn Period

Pay heed to your parents' birthdays. One is happy to
offer birthday greetings, but concerned to see they
have aged another year.

Confucius, Spring and Autumn Period

A gentleman would rescue a man trapped in a well, but he would not jump in himself. He is not perfect, but he is not stupid, either.

Confucius, Spring and Autumn Period

꽃

You can deprive an army of its commander, but you can never deprive a man of his will.

Confucius, Spring and Autumn Period

꽃

The gentlemen will aid others in good deeds, and stay out of trouble. The petty man will do the exact opposite.

Confucius, Spring and Autumn Period

꽃

Honor your father and mother. Be noble in your work. Be loyal and honest to your friends. Never, and nowhere, can these laws be broken.

Confucius, Spring and Autumn Period

Cheap meat is bulked with fat.

Traditional

Seek friends who are better than you, not your own kind.

Traditional

If you are true you will know it. For all the good people in your village will like you, and all the bad ones will hate you.

Confucius, Spring and Autumn Period

It is difficult not to complain when one is poor, but easy to be humble when rich.

Confucius, Spring and Autumn Period

Boasts are harder to honor than promises.
Confucius, Spring and Autumn Period

Be correct yourself, before you correct others.
Traditional

Mutual assistance makes mutual success.
Traditional

Beware lest your eyes are bigger than your belly.
Traditional

It is a disgrace for a gentleman's words to be greater than his deeds.

Confucius, Spring and Autumn Period

❀

Repay resentment with justice. Repay virtue with virtue.

Confucius, Spring and Autumn Period

❀

There is no red gold. There is no perfect man.

Traditional

❀

True friendship is clear like water.
False friendship is sweet, like honey.

Traditional

A great man is hard on himself. A small man is hard on others.

Confucius, Spring and Autumn Period

Do not let your eyes grow on your forehead.
(Don't look down on others)

Traditional

Man's life brings more bitterness than joy
Do what you can while you are young
Help your friends, acquaintances employ
And drink, make haste, before your life is done.

Bao Zhao, Northern Wei Dynasty

I have seen people drown and burn, but I have never seem anyone harmed by doing what is right.

Confucius, Spring and Autumn Period

A man's time has passed if he is despised at forty.

Confucius, Spring and Autumn Period

Overpolite is underhand.

Traditional

A man should fear renown like a pig fears succulence.

Cao Xueqin, Qing Dynasty

Criticism and judgment draw misery upon oneself.

Zhuang Zi, Warring States Period

Praise is only worthwhile when it comes from someone else.

Zhuang Zi, Warring States Period

❀

These are the four abuses: desire to succeed in order to make oneself famous; taking credit for the labors of others; refusal to correct one's errors despite advice; refusal to change one's ideas despite warnings.

Confucius, Spring and Autumn Period

❀

The wise man never trusts in appearances.

Confucius, Spring and Autumn Period

The wise man puts himself last and finds himself first.

Lao Zi, Spring and Autumn Period

Bright sun and moon, shine upon the earth,
Upon this ruthless man without honor.

"Sun & Moon," a song of an abandoned wife from the
Book of Songs, Zhou Dynasty

Take heed of good clothing, and then respect the man.
(Sometimes you can judge by appearances after all...)

Traditional

Why mope, why sigh, why sit and grieve?
Just pour some wine to bring you cheer
Toast your health and sing some songs
The human heart is not of stone
And yet my voice is quiet, alone
My sorrow will escape, I fear

Bao Zhao, Northern Wei Dynasty

One family does not know another's affairs.

Traditional

A son should not live under the same sky with his father's murderer.

Book of Rites, Zhou Dynasty

Creatures of the same nature seek one another.
(Equivalent to "Birds of a feather flock together")
Book of Changes, Zhou Dynasty

Take me, I'm fat. My brother is so thin after all.
Zhao Xiao saves Zhao Li from bandits,
Later Han Dynasty

I prefer natural wings, which good brothers are to any man.
Emperor Wen prefers family loyalty to
sorcerous flight, Wei Dynasty

A tiger does not take insults from sheep.
Traditional

Others leave riches to their children. I leave an unsullied reputation.

Xu Mian, Liang Dynasty

How can a superior man be content to brood like a hen? He should certainly want to fly like a cock.

Zhao Wen, Later Han Dynasty

How sad it is to find no one of like mind.

Xie Lingyun, Eastern Jin Dynasty

When one is mindful of one's distant home,
How can black hair not go gray?

Xie Tao, Northern Wei Dynasty

The caged bird yearns for the forest.

Tao Qian, Eastern Jin Dynasty

Suddenly, I hear an old song,
Weeping, I wish for my home.

Du Shenyen, Tang Dynasty

I wave you off,
Your horse cries for both of us.

Li Bo, Tang Dynasty

Exaggerations carry with them a cartload of demons.

Book of Changes, Zhou Dynasty

Do not be a slave to hoarding money.

Ma Yuan, Later Han Dynasty

※

The young should respect their elders above all things.

Confucius, Spring and Autumn Period

※

In wisdom desire roundness, and in conduct, desire squareness.

Liu Su, Tang Dynasty

※

I have disgraced you by receiving your ornate calligraphy.

Traditional thanks for sending a letter

※

May you early bestow a precious sound.

Traditional request for a letter by return

Do not make the news of you as rare as gold and gems.

Traditional way of saying "Write soon"

I am already obliged for your golden promise.

Traditional thanks for a favor

I am much obliged for being held by the ears and instructed to my face.

Traditional thanks for advice

Many thanks for pushing my wheel.

Traditional thanks for a recommendation

I trust that you will move your precious steps.
Traditional invitation to pop round for a chat

I hope you will act as collar and sleeve.
*Traditional expression for relying on another
to take the lead*

I hope that you will remove the weeds that obstruct
my mind.
Traditional request for instruction or guidance

Your kindness is engraved on my bones.
Traditional expression for "thanks (a lot)"

If later generations call me the penniless magistrate, will that not be a rich inheritance for my descendants.

Yang Zhen refuses to flaunt his wealth, Han Dynasty

He who does good hands down a fair name for a hundred generations; he who does evil hands down a bad name for thousands of years.

Fan Xuanling speaks of the evil that men do,
Southern and Northern Dynasties

Who would let another man snore beside his own couch?

Tai Zi, Song Dynasty

Do not forget great kindness, even for a single meal.

Emperor Wen Di, Han Dynasty

Stoop if the roof is low.

Traditional

The firm, the enduring, the simple and the modest are near to virtue.

Confucius, Spring and Autumn Period

The man who in the view of gain thinks of righteousness, who in the view of danger is prepared to give up his life, and who does not forget an old agreement however far back it extends, such a man may be reckoned a complete man.

Confucius, Spring and Autumn Period.

He who speaks without modesty will find it difficult to make his words good.

Confucius, Spring and Autumn Period

Do not treat others as you yourself would not be treated.

Confucius, Spring and Autumn Period

Five things everywhere under heaven constitute perfect virtue. They are gravity, generosity of soul, sincerity, earnestness and kindness.

Confucius, Spring and Autumn Period

The leader who seeks no personal fame, and has no thought of his own punishment if forced to withdraw, but who lives to protect the people and serve the needs of his sovereign, is the precious jewel of the state.

Sun Zi, Spring and Autumn Period

The leader must be at the forefront of the army's struggles. He neither sits in the shade in summer, nor dons warm clothing in the winter.

Zhang Yu, Song Dynasty

We'd talk and laugh, and think not of going home.

Wang Wei, Tang Dynasty

❀

Let's take another bottle of wine,
And discuss literature in great detail.

Du Fu, Tang Dynasty

❀

Low on cash, I must be satisfied with home brew for
    wine,
I can toast the health of my next-door neighbor,
Over the fence I call: "Bring another cup!"

Du Fu, Tang Dynasty

❀

Bamboo will bend in the wind.
(i.e. it will change with the times, not break)

Traditional

Yesterday did not stay.

Li Bo, Tang Dynasty

I hold up my drink to drown my sorrow, sorrow,
Man will always struggle to live in this world.
Tomorrow, we must let our hair down, and go
    boating.

Li Bo, Tang Dynasty

Loyalty is difficult to express.

Li Bo, Tang Dynasty

Yellow gold and white jade buys song and laughter,
Drunk for many months, with no thought of one's
lord.

Li Bo, Tang Dynasty

I send you this letter across a thousand miles of longing

Li Bo to his old friend Yen, Tang Dynasty

✽

Before the door, your footprints are overgrown with moss.

Li Bo, Tang Dynasty

✽

Drinking till dazed, the country boys forget themselves.

Lu Zhi, Yuan Dynasty

✽

Not enough wine; we go to buy, through miles of moonlight.

Yao Sui, Yuan Dynasty

Men, when suffering injustice, will speak out.

Han Wen'gong, Han Dynasty

My friends are estranged, or far distant,
I bow my head and stand still.

Tao Qian, Eastern Jin Dynasty

"He travels strange roads," I think, among other
things.

Cao Pi, Han Dynasty

Often we have said goodbye to each other. Before,
when I left, the snow seemed to be flowers. Today, I
come back and the flowers seem to be snow.

Fan Yun, Southern and Northern Dynasties

[When the sun rises on a party] beaded blinds become another sea of stars.

Gu Kuang, Tang Dynasty

It is easier to go up the mountain and catch a tiger than to open your mouth and ask for help.

Liu Zunjian (attrib.), Song Dynasty

Glorify virtue and censure vice.

Tang Menglai, Qing Dynasty

The gentleman first practices what he preaches and then preaches what he practices.

Confucius, Spring and Autumn Period

If a ruler himself is upright, all will go well without orders. But if he himself is not upright, even though he gives orders, they will not be obeyed.

Confucius, Spring and Autumn Period

Elevation of the worthy is the foundation of government.

Mo Zi, Warring States Period

The worthy leader starts the day early and retires late.

Mo Zi, Warring States Period

A cold man cannot be choosy about clothes.

Traditional

Be a leader, not a master.

Lao Zi, Spring and Autumn Period

Unconstructive criticism is like trying to stop a flood with water, or fighting fire with fire.

Mo Zi, Warring States Period

One who obeys the will of Heaven will practice universal love.

Mo Zi, Warring States Period

Name is but an accessory of reality.

Xu Yu to Emperor Yao, c. 2300 BC

If you wait for people to lapse into crime and then punish them, it is like placing traps for them. How can a humane ruler countenance placing traps for his subjects?

Mencius, Warring States Period

A gentleman does not bear a grudge.

Traditional

Straight wood does not require the carpenter's tools.

Xun Zi, Warring States Period

From the fact that men are born with desires and when these desires are not satisified, men are bound to pursue their satisfaction. When the pursuit is carried on unrestrained and unlimited, there is bound to be contention.

Xun Zi, Warring States Period

The gentleman acts according to the situation he is in, and does not desire what is outside of it. If he is wealthy and honorable, he acts like one wealthy and honorable. If he is poor and lowly, he acts like one poor and lowly.

Zi Si, Warring States Period

In the archer there is a resemblance to the gentleman. When he misses the mark, he turns and seeks the reason for his failure in himself.

Confucius (attrib.), Spring and Autumn Period

He who strives after truth, chooses the good and holds fast to it.

Zi Si, Warring States Period

If only good men were appointed to office, there would not be enough.

Han Fei Zi, Warring States Period

If a light offense is heavily punished, just imagine the penalty for a serious crime. Thus the people will not dare to break the laws.

Li Si, Warring States Period

If we try to flee, we will die. If we start a revolt, we will also die. Since we die in either case, would it not be better to die fighting for a kingdom?

Chen She to Wu Guang, Qin Dynasty

It is bad luck to kill those who have already surrendered.

Liu Bang, Qin Dynasty

The position of Emperor may only go to a worthy man; it cannot be claimed by empty words and vain talk. I do not dare to take such a position.

Liu Bang, the future First Emperor of Han, Qin Dynasty

Lay not a corpse at someone else's door.

Traditional

One should not expect gratitude when bestowing kindness.

Traditional

Humanity means loving men. Righteousness means respecting the aged.

Ying Tang, attrib. Dong Zhongshu, Han Dynasty

The wise man does not stand beneath a collapsing wall.

Traditional

Filial piety begins with the serving of your parents; next you must serve your sovereign; and finally you must make something of yourself, that your name may go down through the ages to the glory of your father and mother.

Sima Tan, Han Dynasty

The rich start from savings combined.

Traditional

The brave man does not always die for honor; nor does the coward always neglect his duty.

Sima Qian, Han Dynasty

Too numerous to record are the men of ancient times who were rich and noble and whose names have yet vanished away.

Sima Qian, Han Dynasty

Do as a thirsty person drinking from a river. He drinks happily enough, but does not covet the voluminous flow . . . This is how the gentleman exercises his mind for he regards rank and position as a tumor and material wealth as dirt and dust. What is the use of wealth and honor to him?

Xi Kang, Han Dynasty

Failure lies not in falling down, but in not getting up.

Traditional

❦

Of life and property, which is worth more?

Lao Zi, Spring and Autumn Period

❦

A monk does not bow down before a king.

Hui Yuan, Eastern Jin Dynasty

❦

Good invites a pleasant reward, while evil brings about suffering as a result.

Zhi Cang, Sui Dynasty

Every crime will tell its tale upon the day of judgment.

Traditional

I like fish and I also like bear's paws. If I cannot have both I will forgo the fish and take the bear's paws. Similarly, I like living and I like doing my duty to my neighbor; but if I cannot do both, I will forgo my life in preference to doing my duty.

Mencius, Warring States Period

If you bow at all, bow low.

Traditional

Gold is tested by fire, man by gold.

Traditional

To the good be good. To the bad be good, too, in order to make them good as well.

Lao Zi, Spring and Autumn Period

❀

A paper tiger is not so fierce.

Traditional

❀

When a man's trangressions are great, three hundred days are taken away from his term of life. When they are small, three days are taken away. Great and small transgressions number in the hundreds. Those who seek everlasting life on earth must first of all avoid them.

Anon, The Treatise of the Most Exalted One, probably Song Dynasty

No fear I'll fail to pay for wine,
Within the purse the coins are mine.

He Zhizhang, Tang Dynasty

Xu still can give a robe in sympathy
To pity Fan who looks exceeding cold.
Xu knows him not a minister of state,
But takes him for the same poor friend of old.

Gao Shi, Tang Dynasty

But ere we finish what we have to say,
The setting sun will part again our way.

Qian Chi, Tang Dynasty

Then fill, kind host, your guests with wine to
overflow,
That we may always feel at home where'er we go.

Li Bo, Tang Dynasty

Fame is empty.

Tao Qian, Eastern Jin Dynasty

This is something I can only confide to a person of
intelligence; it would not do to speak of it to the
vulgar crowd.

Sima Qian, Han Dynasty

Now the dullard gains favor and fame
The slanderer and the toady have their way.

Jia Yi, Han Dynasty

The shining virtue of the sage must shut itself far
from the filth of the world.

Jia Yi, Han Dynasty

Where is the Prince of Chao, what has he left
But an old castle moat where tadpoles breed?
Those three thousand knights that sat at his board,
Is there one among them whose name is still known?
Let us make merry, get something in our own day
To set against the pity of ages still unborn.

Li Bo, Tang Dynasty

Do not squander gold like earth.

Traditional

Chapter 3

WORK & WISDOM

It is, indeed, a wise man who knows how little he knows. But the Chinese have always attached great value to intellectual accomplishment. One reason for this is the nature of the "decaying nobility." Although many translations use the titles of hereditary peers, such as Duke, Marquis and Count, when discussing historical figures, the true situation was slightly different. Even officials of high rank were liable to see their powers erode over time; because one's father was a Duke it did not follow that one would inherit the title. Instead, the power of a peerage was liable to decline over the generations until the great-great-great-grandchildren of a noble became equivalent in rank to the masses. The only chance of maintaining the family honor was by doing great deeds to gain promotion once more, and the only way of attracting the Emperor's attention, especially in a time of peace, was by passing the rigorous civil service examinations.

Study, especially of the Classics, became of ultimate importance, both for nobles seeking to remain in their positions, and for commoners who coveted the peerage for themselves. Education became a tradition of duty, obligation, hard work and the accumulation of wisdom. In the harsh light of day, some of the "wise words" imparted are still deep and meaningful; others look like old wives' tales. All of them were classed as some sort of wisdom, at some time during China's long history.

The green of grass as seen afar is gone when near.

Han Yu, Tang Dynasty

❀

One look is worth a thousand rumors.

Wen Hou, Warring States Period

❀

Distant water cannot quench a fire close at hand.

Li Chu, Spring and Autumn Period

❀

To catch the tiger's cub, one must enter the tiger's den.

Ban Chao, Eastern Han Dynasty

❀

Let not the opportunity pass, for it may not return.

Kuai Tong, Western Han Dynasty

Even the hardiest plant will not flourish if left in the cold for ten days out of every eleven.

Mencius, Warring States Period

✳

A coin a day makes a thousand coins in a thousand days. In time, a rope may saw through a tree, and dripping water can wear away stone.

Zhang Guiya, Southern Song Dynasty

✳

Do not use firewood to put out a fire.

Minister Su Dai advises Prince Anxi against appeasing the invaders, Warring States Period

Before I begin, I rest my mind and expel all distractions. Then I go to the mountain forest and select the best wood. Then I keep my mind on my work. That is the secret of good furniture.

Qing the carpenter stops to give the king a silly answer to a silly question, Spring and Autumn Period

✺

Does a nurse wrap a baby upside down after thirty years on the job?

Miao Zhen warns the Prime Minister not to teach him to suck eggs, Song Dynasty

✺

What's done is done, it does not require explanation. What's finished need not be interfered with. What's past cannot be remade, there is no point in fixing the blame.

Confucius asks for bygones to be bygones, Spring and Autumn Period

See how contentedly the carp drift through the water.
This is what makes the fish happy.

Zhuang Zi, Warring States Period.

How do you know what the fish think? You're not a
fish.

Hui Zi, Warring States Period.

How do you know what I don't know? You're not me.

Zhuang Zi gets testy, Warring States Period

I'm not you. But you're not a fish either.

Hui Zi refuses to let it lie, Warring States Period

Well why are you asking me, then? They look happy enough to me.

Zhuang Zi gets into deep water, Warring States Period

If you have a knot in silk, tugging will only make it tighter. If two men are fighting, interfering will only make it worse.

Sun Bin, Warring States Period

Who cannot sail a ship when the sea is calm?

Traditional

When people talk of a ferocious tiger, the listeners
are frightened. But none is so frightened as the man
who has suffered a tiger attack in the past.

*Cheng Yi reminds us that nothing beats personal
experience, Northern Song Dynasty*

So you want to rule the world? That is like climbing a
tree to look for fish. It is impossible.

Mencius talks King Xuan out of it, Warring States Period

Look not for the donkey you are sitting on.

Dao Yuan, Song Dynasty

What you speak of is superstition. I speak only the truth. Using your word against mine is like hurling an egg against a rock

Mo Zi does not take kindly to the predictions of a
fortune-teller, Warring States Period

※

Truth is oft disguised as jest.

Traditional

※

Dying embers can still start a fire.

The incarcerated Han Anguo isn't beaten yet,
Western Han Dynasty

※

If there's a fire, I can put it out by pissing on it.

Tian Ji, Han Anguo's prison warden, is not convinced,
Western Han Dynasty

Here's your chance, piss away.

The very tall and imposing Han Anguo to Tian Ji on
his release, Western Han Dynasty

Only when you know why you have hit the target, can you truly say you have learned archery.

Guan Yinzi, Warring States Period

The cunning rabbit has three bolt-holes.

Feng Xuan, Warring States Period

Find enlightenment through heeding many points of view. Find ignorance through heeding few.

Wei Zheng, Tang Dynasty

Pigs and dogs are reared for a purpose. For what use do you rear your disciples?

Deng Xi, Zhou Dynasty

You are only playing a single note. You should find others who can teach you how to use the other holes in your intellectual flute.

Zi Yu accuses Prince Mou of having a one-track mind,
Zhou Dynasty.

After the long slumber of ignorance, a single word can change a man forever.

Nan Guo Zi, Zhou Dynasty

Who can comprehend the motives of Heaven?

Lao Zi, Spring and Autumn Period

People differ in life, but not in death.

Yang Zhu, Zhou Dyasty

Fish big enough to swallow a boat are not found in ditches.

*Yang Zhu refuses to be a big fish in a little pond,
Zhou Dynasty*

The higher the rank I attain, the more humbly I behave. The greater my power, the less I exercise it. The richer my wealth, the more I give away. Thus I avoid envy, spite and misery.

Sun Shu Ao, Zhou Dynasty

Two small creatures chatter about matters they cannot understand. A small brain cannot comprehend the workings of a great mind.

Zhuang Zi, Warring States Period

The blind cannot see, for they have no eyes. The deaf cannot hear, for they have no ears. You do not understand, for you have no spirit.

Lian Shu to the doubting Jian Wu, Zhou Dynasty

Your words are meaningful, but have no practical value.

Hui Zi to Zhuang Zi, Warring States Period

Everything useful perishes through use . . . Should I
not rejoice at being useless?

Zhuang Zi to Hui Zi, Warring States Period

I am no more impressed by your apologies than I was
by your accusations.

Lao Zi rebukes the insolent Shi Cheng Qi,
Spring and Autumn Period

Geese are white, crows are black. No argument will
change this.

Lao Zi, Spring and Autumn Period

If a man values his wife's virtue above her looks, serves his parents to the best of his ability, is prepared to lay down his life for his lord and keeps his promises to his friends, I would judge that he is most learned, though he may never have been to school.

Zi Xia, Spring and Autumn Period

Do not worry if others do not understand you. Worry if you do not understand them.

Confucius, Spring and Autumn Period

Reading without thinking will confuse you.
Thinking without reading will place you in danger.

Confucius, Spring and Autumn Period

He who learns the truth of everything in the morning, can die happy in the evening.

Confucius believes studies are never done, Spring and Autumn Period

It is not that I do not like your teachings, just that I do not have the energy to follow them.

Ran Qiu to Confucius, Spring and Autumn Period

If it were down to energy, you could rest halfway. But you have not even taken the first step.

Confucius to Ran Qiu, Spring and Autumn Period

Some seeds sprout but never bloom. Some bloom but never bear fruit.

Confucius, Spring and Autumn Period

Only in winter do the pine and cypress show they are evergreen.

Confucius points out that all trees are green when times are easy, Spring and Autumn Period

Drink wine by all means, but do not get drunk.

Confucius, Spring and Autumn Period

Tiger, leopard, dog and sheep. They all look the same without their hair.

Zi Gong, Spring and Autumn Period

My Master speaks only when he has something to say, laughs only when happy, takes only what is needed. This way he angers nobody.

Gongming Jia, Spring and Autumn Period

In olden times, people studied to improve themselves. Today, they only study to impress others.

Confucius, Spring and Autumn Period

A virtuous man concentrates on his own work, not that of others.

Zengzi, Spring and Autumn Period

Everyone is entitled to an education

Confucius, Spring and Autumn Period

If you have nowhere else to go, stay where you are.

Zi Lu, Spring and Autumn Period

I hate those who mistake plagiarism for wisdom, who confuse foolhardiness with bravery, and who consider it righteous to meddle in others' private affairs.

Zi Gong, Spring and Autumn Period

Fish live in water. Men die in it.
Nature is diverse, and not all tastes are the same.

Zhuang Zi, Warring States Period

A hungry man will eat anything, a thirsty man will drink anything.

Mencius, Warring States Period

Do not take the seeds and throw away the melon.

Traditional

Do today's work, today.

Traditional

Believing all books is worse than believing none.

Traditional

Get up late and go early to sleep.

Tao Qian, Eastern Jin Dynasty

Flowers cannot remain red for a hundred days.

Traditional

To the thirsty, a single cup of water is like sweet dew.

Traditional

There is always work for the capable man.

Zhuang Zi, Warring States Period

You can lead a cow to water, but you cannot make it drink.

Traditional

The higher the climb, the further the fall.

Traditional

A kind man sees kindness, the wise man sees wisdom.

Book of Changes, Zhou Dynasty

Day by day the past receding
Day by day the future yields
Just outside the gates I'm seeing
Ancient graveyards ploughed for fields
Yue-fu: Nineteen Ancient Poems, Han Dynasty

❀

Failure is the mother of success.

Traditional

❀

Practice makes for true knowledge.

Tuotuo, Yuan Dynasty

❀

Wanting to know everything is the worst of follies.

Zhuang Zi, Warring States Period

❀

To fare well, a man must trust in his feelings.

Zhuang Zi, Warring States Period

A wheel is made of thirty spokes, but it is turned by the axis.

Lao Zi, Spring and Autumn Period

If I give a student one corner of a subject and he cannot find the other three, the lesson is not worth teaching.

Confucius, Spring and Autumn Period

The more laws made, the more criminals created.

Lao Zi, Spring and Autumn Period

Heaven may produce unexpected wind and clouds.
Life may produce unexpected calamities.

Traditional

One arrow scares five boars.

"The Hunter", Book of Songs,
Spring and Autumn Period

Even summers may have winter weather.

Traditional

Better to display your ugliness than to hide your ignorance.

Traditional

Hours and days melt away.

Traditional

※

He who steals a chicken while small, will grow up to steal an ox.

Traditional

※

Woe is me, like tumbleweed, alone in the world,
My roots long-dead, no rest day or night,
Blown east and west down many paths
Blown south and north down countless roads
Whirlwinds blow me up into the clouds
Is this the end? But no, now I'm sunk beneath the
waves

Cao Zhi, Eastern Han Dynasty

A spark of fire may burn a plain.

Traditional

✿

Sheep's wool comes from a sheep's body.

Traditional

✿

No dawn for a thousand years
No wise sage can help them now
Many times we came to mourn
But soon returned, our sorrows done
Relatives, would grieve awhile
Though most already sing again
Where do the dead go after death
Entrusted to the mountain's caves?

Death comes to us all, muses Tao Qian,
Eastern Jin Dynasty

Rosy cheeks fade, twilight draws near
The cold light dims as dusk arrives
Forget your sorrows, calm your thoughts
And hear my song: "The Weary Road"

Bao Zhao, Northern Wei Dynasty

Heaven arches over like a tent
Over the four corners of the steppes
The sky is gray, is gray forever
The wilderness is vast, is vast
The wind bends the grasses
And we see sheep and cattle grazing

Yue-fu, Northern Dynasties

One night I was a butterfly, fluttering happily around. Then I awoke, and found that I was a man. But what am I in truth? A man who dreams he is a butterfly, or a butterfly who dreams he is a man?

Zhuang Zi, Warring States Period

There is no logical reason for this misfortune. Thus it must be part of my destiny.

Zi Sang, Zhou Dynasty

He who has many sons, has many worries. He who is rich, has many troubles. He who lives a long time, suffers many changes in fortune.

Emperor Yao, c. 2300 BC

There are no more wise men.

Lao Zi, Spring and Autumn Period

I go east to the cliff's edge
And gaze upon the blue ocean
See how the water rolls and churns

Cao Cao, Eastern Han Dynasty

How long has the river been flowing?
How long has this mountain been here?
The fate of man is constantly changing.
Only nature lasts forever

Zhan Fangsheng, Eastern Jin Dynasty

I wake to write a new poem
But it slips my mind, and then I feel the sadness of a traveler.

Zhan Fengsheng, Eastern Jin Dynasty

A servant cannot have two masters.

Traditional

Clouds follow the dragon and wind follows the tiger. The wise man appears and other men look to him for guidance.

Book of Changes, Zhou Dyasty

Ice is produced from water, and yet is colder than water.
(The pupil surpasses the teacher)

Xun Zi, Warring States Period

A youth is to be regarded with respect. How do you
know that his future will not be equal to our present?
Confucius, Spring and Autumn Period

The rice unharvested in the fields
What food is there for the master?
I want to serve, to show courage
Like the good soldiers
To be worthy like them
Up at dawn to fight, not back before dark
A farmer is unsure of how best to serve his country,
Yue-fu: Nineteen Ancient Poems, Han Dynasty

The Prince's liking for small waists has caused many
deaths in the palace.
An old song warns against dieting,
Five Dynasties and Ten Kingdoms

By using bronze as a mirror, you can adjust your clothes and hat. By using history as a mirror, you can know the rise and fall of empires. By using man as a mirror, you can know your virtues and errors.

Tai Cong, Tang Dynasty

🕸

Fair and foul plants are placed in different vessels.

Yan Hui, Spring and Autumn Period

🕸

The Emperor never jests.

The Duke of Zhou, Zhou Dynasty

🕸

Do not drive the tiger from the front door, while letting the wolf get in the back.

Hu Zhidang, Han Dynasty

It is not wise for a blind man, riding a blind horse at midnight, to approach the brink of a deep pond.

Traditional warning to stay away from thin ice

❦

When you aim at the rat, beware of the vase.

Traditional

❦

Porcelain dogs do not keep watch at night, nor do earthenware cocks crow at dawn.

Emperor Yuan Di, Liang Dynasty

❦

An author's literary productions should be his own, and in form and style should constitute a style of their own. How can an author be content to be as others are?

Zu Rong, Northern Wei Dynasty

Go not ahead with nothing in front.

Traditional

Once a word is spoken, four horses cannot drag it back.

Ouyang Xiu, Song Dynasty

The plan of the day is made in the morning.

Traditional

Do not mourn the people of the past, they are gone.

Xie Lingyun, Eastern Jin Dynasty

I followed the mountains for a thousand miles
Drifted downstream these ten nights past,
Resting the oars as the birds return,
The stars thin out above our weary band,
The Moon still shines in the morning,
Cold, so cold, the early morning dew.

Xie Lingyun, Eastern Jin Dynasty

茶

The Moon sinks, like a mirror in the sky.

Li Bo, Tang Dynasty

茶

A student of talent and virtue will pursue his studies single-mindedly, with no thought of other distractions at college.

Book of Rites, Zhou Dynasty

Does a mirror ever tire of reflecting?
Does a clear stream ever tire of the gentle breeze?
Yuan Yang, Northern and Southern Dynasty

❀

Open a book and you are profited.
Emperor Tai Cong, Song Dynasty

❀

Not having studied, he was destitute of skill.
Ban Gu is not impressed with Ho Guang, Han Dynasty

❀

For fifty years men have been worthless, but within a
thousand square leagues, heaven was not completely
barren.
Liu To expresses his thanks for passing the Imperial
examinations, Han Dynasty

A great scholar stands a head above the others.
Ouyang Xiu is impressed with Su Shi, Song Dynasty

Examinations are a deadly struggle in the thorny enclosure.
Traditional

The carriage wheels are free for a journey to the clouds.
Traditional congratulation upon gaining a degree

❀

Do not open your clothes to embrace the fire.
Traditional

Do not ask the way from a blind man.

Han Wen'gong, Han Dynasty

✿

Your Imperial Majesty does not relish the many delicious dishes, nor value your precious body. Instead, you resign yourself to the morbid love of wine and excessive passion for women. This is like cutting one tree with both axes, and it will be exceptional indeed if the tree does not fall.

Oshabuhua warns Emperor Wu against burning the candle at both ends, Yuan Dynasty

✿

Hear all sides and you will be enlightened. Hear one side, and you will be in the dark.

Wei Zheng to Emperor Tai Cong, Tang Dynasty

The nimble foot gets in first.

Kuai Tung, Zhou Dynasty

Anything great is long in making.

Lao Zi, Spring and Autumn Period

Do not solely peruse the books of your father.

Lin Xiangru advises keeping up with the times,
Zhou Dynasty

Even the wise man makes mistakes. Even the fool is sometimes right.

Guang Wu to Han Xin, Zhou Dynasty

Fortune-telling is a means of setting doubts at rest. If there are no doubts, why tell fortunes?

Dou Lian, Zhou Dynasty

Man cannot avoid death and disease.

Wen Zhuang, Ming Dynasty

You cannot have a good horse that doesn't eat grass.

Mencius, Warring States Period

An untutored man is like uncarved jade.

Book of Rites, Zhou Dynasty

Red clouds at morning, will not last till afternoon
Red clouds at night, the sunshine will crack the earth

Traditional

He knows most who says he knows least.

Confucius, Spring and Autumn Period

Do not stand by a tree stump waiting for a hare.

Han Fei Zi, Spring and Autumn Period

Those who wear the silk do not rear the worms.

Traditional

When you have faults, do not fear to abandon them.

Confucius, Spring and Autumn Period

The wise man does not set his mind either for anything or against anything; what is right, he will follow.

Confucius, Spring and Autumn Period

The cautious seldom err.

Confucius, Spring and Autumn Period

The wise man is satisfied and composed; the mean man is always full of distress.

Confucius, Spring and Autumn Period

While you do not know life, how can you know about death?

Confucius, Spring and Autumn Period

❋

Going too far is as wrong as falling short.

Confucius, Spring and Autumn Period

❋

The scholar who cherishes the love of comfort is not fit to be deemed a scholar.

Confucius, Spring and Autumn Period

❋

The wise man is distressed by his want of ability.

Confucius, Spring and Autumn Period

There are three things against which the wise man guards: lust when young, quarrels when strong, and covetousness when old.

Confucius, Spring and Autumn Period

Manifest plainness, embrace simplicity, reduce selfishness, have few desires.

Lao Zi, Spring and Autumn Period

He who knows does not speak. He who speaks does not know.

Lao Zi, Spring and Autumn Period

Heaven's net is indeed vast. Though its meshes are wide, it misses nothing.

Lao Zi, Spring and Autumn Period.

True words are not beautiful. Beautiful words are not true. A good man does not argue. He who argues is not a good man.

Lao Zi, Spring and Autumn Period

He who pursues fame at the risk of losing his self is not a scholar.

Zhuang Zi, Warring States Period

The painters of today mix their brushes and ink with dust and dirt, and their colors with mud, and smear the silk in vain. How can this be called painting?

Zhang Yenyuan, Tang Dynasty

Woman is superior to man in the same respect as water is superior to fire.

Records of the Bedchamber, Sui Dynasty

❀

A child conceived during daytime will be given to vomiting.

Records of the Bedchamber, Sui Dynasty

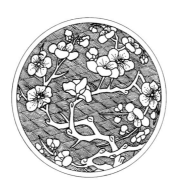

A child conceived at midnight will be either mute, deaf or blind.

Records of the Bedchamber, Sui Dynasty

A child conceived during a solar eclipse will be either burned or wounded.

Records of the Bedchamber, Sui Dynasty

A child conceived during a thunderstorm will easily develop mental troubles.

Records of the Bedchamber, Sui Dynasty

A child conceived during a lunar eclipse will be persecuted by an ill fate, and so will its mother.

Records of the Bedchamber, Sui Dynasty

A child conceived when there is a rainbow in the sky will be exposed to ill fortune.

Records of the Bedchamber, Sui Dynasty

🦋

A child conceived during the solstice will bring harm to its parents.

Records of the Bedchamber, Sui Dynasty

🦋

A child conceived when the moon is waxing or waning will be killed in the war or blinded by the wind.

Records of the Bedchamber, Sui Dynasty

A child conceived while drunk or overfed, will suffer from epilepsy, boils and ulcers.

Records of the Bedchamber, Sui Dynasty

Until a man reaches forty, he is usually full of vigorous passion. But as soon as he has passed his fortieth year, he will suddenly notice that his potency is decreasing.

Sun Zimo, Tang Dynasty

When drunk, the truth tumbles out.

Traditional

One hundred rivers return to the sea.
(i.e. all roads lead to Rome)

Traditional

✺

One day's cold will not freeze you in three feet of ice.

Traditional

✺

Autumn clouds darken overhead
How many, so many . . .

Li Bo, Tang Dynasty

✺

Ups and downs are already settled.
There is no need to ask a fortune-teller.

Li Bo, Tang Dynasty

Shade and light are different in every valley.

Li Bo, Tang Dynasty

Sometimes I'd walk, walk far from home,
The things I've seen, and I alone.

Wang Wei, Tang Dynasty

Tomorrow morning I have business to attend to,
Many times I ask the night, what shall I do?

Du Fu, Tang Dynasty

Spring silkworms spin their silk and die.

Li Shangyin warns against complacency,
Tang Dynasty

There may be no men on the mountain,
But voices of men can be heard.

Wang Wei, Tang Dynasty

❀

Alone I sit amid the dark bamboo
Playing my lute and whistling a song
No man knows I am in the deep forest
Only the shining Moon comes to visit.

Wang Wei, Tang Dynasty

❀

The sun sets and the traveler mourns.

Meng Haoran, Tang Dynasty

❀

The merchant's daughters do not understand the
grief of a lost kingdom.

Du Mu, Tang Dynasty

I take my sword to cut the water; water still flows.

Li Bo, Tang Dynasty

᭱

Nature and feelings are born of habit.

Li Bo, Tang Dynasty

᭱

Stand upon the highest ridge, and see, how small the other mountains seem.

Du Fu, Tang Dynasty

᭱

The past, the present, where do they end?
A thousand years are gone with the wind.

Li He, Tang Dynasty

Play is a gift from heaven, work is a man-made ill.

Liu Zhi, Yuan Dynasty

A path along a stream is full of peril.

Zhang Kejiu, Yuan Dynasty

Grab, and something will slip through your fingers.

Lao Zi, Spring and Autumn Period

Although the rivers and mountains of the world have not changed, their ancient and modern names are different.

Wen Zhuang, Ming Dynasty

Only country bumpkins cannot read.

Wen Zhuang, Ming Dynasty

Beware an ear laid close to the wall.
(i.e. walls have ears)

Book of Songs, Zhou Dynasty

Do not forget to take your wife when you move house.

Traditional

Orchids have a fragrance fit for a king.

Confucius, Spring and Autumn Period

There is a time for all things. The chrysanthemum in autumn and the peach blossom in spring.

Wen Zhuang, Ming Dynasty

Onflowing streams whirl and fall, without plan, to east or west.

Wu Qun, Southern and Northern Dynasties

Cicadas invent a thousand tunes, without tiring.

Wu Qun, Southern and Northern Dynasties

One tree does not make a forest.

Traditional

[The view is so good that] We cannot fully, by day's end admire.

Du Fu, Tang Dynasty

❀

This is another sky. No likeness to the human world below.

Li Bo, Tang Dynasty

❀

Jealousy arises often from a narrow heart.

Traditional

❀

A fish that frees itself from a hook, will swim away, never to return.

Traditional

When fortune flees even gold loses its luster
When fortune returns even iron shines bright.

Traditional

✱

The beauties of the Han Dynasty and Tang Dynasty
end in common dust.

Xin Chizhi, Kin Dynasty

✱

You know the music of Earth, but you have not heard
the music of Heaven.

Zhuang Zi, Warring States Period

None knows what will happen from one day to the next.

Guan Hanching, Yuan Dynasty

There are some things which possess form but are devoid of sound, as, for instance, jade and stone. Other have sound, but are without form, such as wind and thunder. Others again have form and sound, such as men and animals. Lastly, there is a class devoid of both, namely devils and spirits.

Han Wen'gong, Han Dynasty

Personally, I disbelieve in the irregularity of natural phenomena, and regard as evil spirits only those who injure their neighbors.

Tang Menglai, Qing Dynasty

Though their clothes are too tattered to keep out the
  cold,
They'll assure you they change all base metals to gold.
An anonymous warning against alchemists,
Ming Dynasty

The creature born is the creature dying.
Zhuang Zi, Warring States Period

You are too hasty in forming your estimate. You see
an egg, and expect to see it crow. You look at the
crossbow, and expect to see a dove roasting.
Chang Wu to Chu Qiao, Warring States Period

There are always people who speak when there is no need to speak, and weep when there is no need to weep ... This is what the ancients called the crime of violating the principle of Nature. The Master came because it was his natural time; he went because it was his natural course.

Qin Shi on the death of Lao Zi,
Spring and Autumn Period

A battering ram can knock down a city wall, but it cannot stop a hole. Different things have different uses.

Zhuang Zi, Warring States Period

The life of things passes by like a galloping horse.
Zhuang Zi, Warring States Period

Every movement brings a change, every hour makes a difference.

Zhuang Zi, Warring States Period

❀

Do not let the artificial destroy the natural; do not let effort destroy destiny, do not sacrifice fun for fame.

Zhuang Zi, Warring States Period

❀

They were able to subdue people's tongues, but not to win their hearts. Such is the weakness of a pedant.

Zhuang Zi on Huan Tuan and Gong-sun Lun,
Warring States Period

❀

Heaven does not cancel Winter because men dislike cold.

Xun Zi, Warring States Period

The King of Chu has a thousand chariots followig
him. This is not because he is wise.

Xun Zi, Warring States Period

❦

You look upon the seasons with expectation and await
them: why not seize the seasonal opportunities and
exploit them?

Xun Zi, Warring States Period

❦

The nature of man is evil; his goodness is acquired.

Xun Zi, Warring States Period

❦

Among barbarians, act like a barbarian.

Zi Si, Warring States Period

Claiming certainty without corroborating evidence is stupid.

Han Fei Zi, Warring States Period

❀

Farming is hard work. And yet people do it because they think it will make them rich.

Han Fei Zi, Warring States Period

❀

If one man does not work the fields, another goes hungry.

Emperor Wu Cong, Tang Dynasty

❀

He who waits on others misses his opportunities.

Li Si, Warring States Period

This is the one moment in ten thousand ages.
Li Si, Warring States Period

All things depart from that which is different from themselves, and follow that which is the same.
Dong Zhongshu, Han Dynasty

Men have their tasks and women their hearths.
Confucius, Spring and Autumn Period

Scarcity creates value. Plenty creates complacency.
Traditional

If they eat human beings, what is to stop them eating me?

Lu Xun, Diary of a Madman,
Qing Dynasty/Republican Period

Life is but a smile on the lips of death.

Li Zhinfa, People's Republic

When you have wealth, why should you strive for more?

Traditional

Even oceans may at last run dry.

Traditional

I grieve that I have things in my heart that I am not able to express fully, and that I am shamed to think that after I am gone my writings will not be known to posterity.

Sima Qian, Han Dynasty

The blacker the wok, the better the cook.

Traditional

With a strong heart and a ready mind
What have I to fear?
Since I know there is no escape from death,
Let me not cling to a foolish love of life.

Chu Yuan, Zhou Dynasty

If you stop and confine yourself to one place, you will develop prejudices.

Guo Xiang, Han Dynasty

✱

Even if we were endowed with the sharpest sense of hearing, we could not hear all the sounds there are.

Ge Hung, Han Dynasty

✱

Should one say that something does not exist, merely because we have never seen or heard of it?

Ge Hung, Han Dynasty

✱

The coward has a dream, the brave man has a vision.

Traditional

The spirit never perishes, only the body decays.

> *Mou Zi, Southern and Northern Dynasties*

I have quoted those things, sir, which I knew you would understand. Had I preached the words of the Buddhist scripture or discussed the essence of non-action, it would have been like speaking to a blind man of the five colors, or playing the five sounds to a deaf man.

> *Mou Zi drags himself down to his critics' level,*
> *Southern and Northern Dynasties*

What is spirit? It is subtlety that has reached the extreme and become immaterial.

Hui Yuan, Eastern Jin Dynasty

❀

Obey heaven to prosper.

Traditional

❀

Everything creaeted and non-created, everything seemingly real or unreal, is all inseparable from consciousness.

Xuan Zhuang, Sui/Tang Dynasty

❀

Have not a tiger's head with a snake's tail.

Traditional

Respect ghosts and spirits, but keep them at a distance.

Confucius, *Spring and Autumn Period*

Feng shui may or may not be based upon sound principles; at any rate, to indulge a morbid belief in it is utter folly.

Pu Songling, Qing Dynasty

Take a man whose third finger is bent and cannot be stretched out straight. It is not painful, neither does it interfere with his work, yet if there were anyone who could make it straight, he would think nothing of journeying such a distance as from Qin to Qu, simply because his finger is not as good as those of other people. But to be grieved because one's finger is not as good as other people's, and not to be grieved because one's heart is not as good as other people's, this is called ignorance of the relative importance of categories.

Mencius, Warring States Period

No medicine is as good as a middling doctor.

Traditional

An idol-maker does not worship the gods: he knows what stuff they are made of.

Traditional

※

Half an orange tastes as sweet as a whole one.

Traditional

※

As fades the spring my days are fading fast.

Ling-hu Chu, Tang Dynasty

※

Beat the grass to frighten the snakes.

Traditional

※

Here rose and fell full many a state,
Like streams that eastward flow – who asks their
    fate?

Xie Yong, Tang Dynasty

Why toil till your hair turns white if none takes heed?

Chen Zi'ang, Tang Dynasty

A bridge never crossed is a life never lived.

Traditional

'Twas here that prince and hero farewell said.
That dauntless hero proudly held his head.
Those valiant men of old have passed away,
Still trembling flows this icy stream today.

Lou Binwang watches the river as time goes by,
Tang Dynasty

All questions have two sides.

Traditional

My ferry-boat, unmanned, must idly turn and swing.
Wei Yingwu, Tang Dynasty

The evening clouds are gone, the air is cool and clear,
The Milky Way is mute, the moon a shining sphere.
This life and lovely night will not last long for me,
Then where shall I another year this bright moon
   see?
Du Mu, Song Dynasty

Much property is a trap for the stupid.
Tao Qian, Eastern Jin Dynasty

[My son] A-Xuan is keen on learning,
But love of letters is not in him.

Tao Qian, Eastern Jin Dynasty

Fame is empty.

Tao Qian, Eastern Jin Dynasty

Those whose ways are different cannot lay plans for one another.

Confucius, Spring and Autumn Period

The stupid man is bound by custom, confined as though in fetters.

Jia Yi, Han Dynasty

When you see a straight piece of wood, you do not want to make it into a wheel.

Each to his own, suggests Xi Kang to Shan Tao,
Han Dynasty

Size is of the least importance. For a giant corpse only feeds more vultures.

Ruan Zhi, Han Dynasty

Making an ax handle requires wood cut with an ax.

Lu Zhi can't win them all, Jin Dynasty

A sour wind impales the eyes.

Li He, Tang Dynasty

One living in blessings does not know it is a blessing.

Traditional

Know deeply the depths and the details.

Traditional

✳

Spare not the tether if it costs you your cow.

Traditional

✳

Those waiting to eat are a big crowd.

Traditional

✳

Misfortunes never come alone.

Traditional

A well may be deep and a rope may be short.

Traditional warning against biting off
more than one can chew

※

It is easy to take a light carriage on a familiar road.

Traditional

※

I hear and forget. I see and I remember. I do and I understand.

Confucius, Spring and Autumn Period

He who asks is a fool for five minutes. But he who does not ask remains a fool forever.

Traditional

Eat less, taste more.

Traditional

A hundred men scrambling to fetch a gourd by cart will accomplish less than one man holding it in his hand.

Ying Hou, Warring States Period

I eat only to live.

The Queen of Zhao, Warring States Period

❀

Do not expose money to eyes.

Traditional

❀

An inch of shade is a foot of jade.

Time is money, warns the Huai Nan Zi, Han Dynasty

❀

Strike the iron while it is still hot.

Traditional

❀

Ding is ding and mao is mao.
(A spade's a spade)

Traditional.

There can still be sun in the east and rain in the west.

Traditional

Whoever says good of me is a thief, whoever says bad of me is my teacher.

Traditional

A ram may get stuck butting a fence.

Traditional

He who takes the life of of even one person still has
to atone for it with his own life; yet is the harm done
by opium limited to the taking of one life only?

Lin Zexu to Queen Victoria, Qing Dynasty

More eating rice, less talking mouth.

Traditional

Chapter 4

LOVE & OTHER EMOTIONS

Just as Chinese political writers often pretended to be discussing the past when they were actually avoiding trouble in the present, romance in China often comes hidden beneath many veils of allusion. Rather than directly express an emotion, it was not uncommon for the Chinese to let the elements do it for them. Entire encyclopedias have been written about the world of Chinese symbolism, but there is very little space to discuss it here. Interested readers are advised to read some of the poems and proverbs in this book in conjunction with the symbolism explained in its companion volume, the Little Book of Feng Shui, which goes some way toward elucidating the best-known references.

Many of the poems and proverbs that follow take on a different meaning, for example, when we discover that the wild goose is a symbol of letters and communication, and to be "trapped among flowers" is to fall in love. "Spring," the season, also means youth and, in some cases, stirrings of love. The most innocent of verses takes on an extra, salacious dimension when we understand that to "make the rain and clouds" is to make love, and that the Chinese characters for "woman" and "eyebrow" combine to mean "flirt."

Some of the poems, while seeming quite harmless, are so loaded with bawdy innuendo that a full explanation would lead this book to be classed as pornography. Find the hidden meanings if you can, but this little book can only cover the simplest of poetical allusions. The really dirty ones will have to rely on your own skills of cryptography.

The gate that gave life to you, can also be the gate that leads to your death.

Anon., Flowers of the Peach Tree in a Golden Vase,
Ming Dynasty

The Yellow Emperor had intercourse with twelve hundred women, and thereby became an immortal. Ordinary men have but one woman, and that is usually enough to kill them.

Records of the Bedchamber, Sui Dynasty

The flowers of the cherry tree
Sway to and fro upon the branch
It's not that I do not miss my love
But her home is far, far away

Traditional

He does not miss her. What would a true lover care about distance?

Confucius is unimpressed, Spring and Autumn Period

Her skin is as tender as congealed lard.

A questionable compliment to the Duchess Zhuang Jiang, Book of Songs, Zhou Dynasty

Seeing each other may be good, but living together can be difficult.

Traditional

A day without her is like three years alone.

Book of Songs, Zhou Dynasty

I wake, I sleep, I think of her
The time so long, the distance far

Book of Songs, Zhou Dynasty

※

Pity the man on Dragon Hill, gossiping all night until he hears the roar of the lioness on the East Bank, catching his breath yet dropping his staff in fear.

Su Dongpo needles his friend Chen Zao about his overbearing wife, Song Dynasty

※

One look from her and a city would surrender. Two looks would defeat the men of an entire nation.

Li Yannian sets his sister up with Emperor Wu, Han Dynasty

The mirror and my wife have gone away,
This shard I have, but not my love.

Xu Deyan, Sui Dynasty

❈

Life is a blessing. Not being born, and not dying at
one's time, these are great misfortunes.

Lie Zi, Zhou Dynasty

❈

After living a hundred years, those who do not die of
sadness, die of boredom.

Yang Zhu, Zhou Dynasty

❈

The wise man prefers life to possessions.

Niu Que, Zhou Dynasty

To love all living things and treat them well, without thought of the self, this is good and just.

Confucius, Spring and Autumn Period

Do not the tiger and the wolf love their children?

Zhuang Zi, Warring States Period

Good looks bring trouble without diplomacy.

Confucius, Spring and Autumn Period

I have never met anyone who loves virtue as much as he loves beauty.

> *Confucius, Spring and Autumn Period*

When she's close she's insolent, when she's far away she nags.

> *Confucius, Spring and Autumn Period*

Wine and wenches cost money.

> *Traditional*

Birds love their nests, men love their homes.

> *Traditional*

Softness overcomes hardness.
> Zuo Qiuming, Spring and Autumn Period

Of all the tools of death, desire has killed the most.
> Zhuang Zi, Warring States Period

When a house is small, the wife and mother-in-law will argue.
> Zhuang Zi, Warring States Period

The love that is not deep is quickly broken.
> Traditional

Crooked southern trees wear their vines with pride,
Brides who please their husbands shine with
happiness.

Book of Songs, Spring and Autumn Period

The light fades from the sun and moon
Sorrow troubles my heart like a stain on my clothes
Silently I wonder: if only I could fly away

Book of Songs, Zhou Dynasty

When I can see you no longer,
My tears fall like rain.

Duchess Zhuang Jiang, Zhou Dynasty

The wind blows savagely,
He talks to me and smiles
  A love blows hot and cold, Book of Songs, Zhou Dynasty

※

"Till death do us us part," but we were parted,
When now can I take your hand, and grow old in peace?
    A soldier thinks of his wife as he marches into battle,
                    Book of Songs, Zhou Dynasty

※

I hear the song of the wild geese,
I see the rising sun,
Will you come back and marry me,
Before the streams freeze over?
                    Book of Songs, Zhou Dynasty
          (An alternate translation for the final line could be
                    "Before the autumn's done?")

A girl, touched by spring
A handsome man seduces her
Book of Songs, Zhou Dynasty

"Let's go a-walking," so says she
"I've been already," answers he
"Then let's go again, you and me."
An amorous girl entices a man down by the river,
Book of Songs, Zhou Dynasty

Walk on, walk on
We must live far apart
Ten thousand miles between us
At opposite ends of the sky
The road is hard and long
Will we ever meet again?
Yue-fu: Nineteen Ancient Poems, Han Dynasty

Green upon green, the river grasses
Leaves upon leaves, the willow garden
Flower of all flowers, the girl in the tower
Shining brightly at her window
Putting rouge upon her lovely face
Once a singer, now she is the wife of a dissolute man
The husband has gone away, never to return
And now she sleeps in an empty bed

Yue-fu: Nineteen Ancient Poems, Han Dynasty

When the mountains fall and crumble
When the rivers cease to flow
When the winter thunder rumbles
When the summer rains bring snow
Only if the sky falls earthward
Would I dare our love forgo
Yue-fu: Nineteen Ancient Poems, Han Dynasty

A brooch, two pearls in tortoiseshell
Entwined with jade, the jeweller's art
Now I hear you have another
Hurt, I twist my gift apart
Burned and broken, wind blows ashes
Never tell who broke my heart
Yue-fu: Nineteen Ancient Poems, Han Dynasty

When she walks by, the men set down their loads and
   smooth their beards
The boys doff their hats and check their hair
The farmer ceases plowing, the gardener looks up
   from his hoe.
   The pretty Lo-fu causes a stir, "On theMulberry Road,"
                                                   Han Dynasty

The governor sends words to Lo-fu: "Would you like
   to come for a ride?"
But she approaches him and says: "How bold you are!
For you are a married man, and I, I might add, am a
   married woman."
   The governor puts his foot in it, "On the Mulberry Road,"
                                                   Han Dynasty

At sunset she came outside
I watched as she walked past
Her face a picture, her hair hiding her eyes
Her perfume already filling the street
Yue-fu: Zi Ye Songs, Southern Dynasties

Last night, her hair unbrushed
Like black silk thrown over her shoulders
As she curled up on her knees
Lovely in every way
Yue-fu: Zi Ye Songs, Southern Dynasties

The night is long, I cannot sleep
The shining Moon gleams in my eyes
I thought I heard someone call my name
In vain, I answer the empty air
Yue-fu: Zi Ye Songs, Southern Dynasties

Fresh flowers shine in the forest
The fish play in the clear stream
At the bank I cast my line
And sit contented, not caring if I catch a fish or not

Wang Binzhi, Eastern Jin Dynasty

When a son is born, what is desired for him is that he may have a wife.

Mencius, Warring States Period

If she does not obey my commands in a small matter like stewing pears, how will she act when the matter is of grave importance?

Zeng Zi divorces his wife, Spring and Autumn Period

When the moonlight glints among the rafters
I reflect on your beauty
When the evening mist shrouds the trees of Spring
I think of you, and watch for your graceful presence

Li Bo, Tang Dynasty

Thy breasts are like the seeds in a newly-opened lotus.

Ming Huang compliments Yang Guifei,
somewhat naughtily, Tang Dynasty

Use the days of plenty to think of days of nothing.

Traditional

Wine and meat brings many "brothers." Times of
trouble bring no one.

Traditional

❀

Sorrow of sorrows, suffering no smile,
Take my hand, and stay a while.

Xie Tao, Northern Wei Dynasty

❀

Steep rocks split the face of heaven,
The woven branches mask the sun,
Spring blossoms fall on the stream in shadow,
Summer snow lies on the cold peaks.

Kong Zhigui, Northern and Southern Dynasties

Suddenly, I hear an old song,
Weeping, I wish for my home.

Du Shenyen, Tang Dynasty

✾

The sun rises from the sea, the night is torn,
On the river, another year away from youth.
Is anyone reading the letters I send home,
Returning, like the geese, to Luoyang.

Wang Wan, Tang Dynasty

✾

Clouds above drift like my thoughts.

Li Bo, Tang Dynasty

✾

Husband and wife are like the phoenixes in their
pairing.

Wen Zhuang, Ming Dynasty

The sound of her silk skirt has stopped,
On the marble pavement dust grows,
Her empty room is cold and still,
Fallen leaves are piled against the doors,
Longing for that lovely lady,
How can I bring my aching heart to rest?
Han Wudi on the death of his mistress, Han Dynasty

Without clouds, there can be no rain.

Traditional

No joy shall equal the delights of our wedding night,
These shall never be forgotten, however old we may
grow.
Zhang Heng's poem of a bride's word to her husband,
Han Dynasty

If a son is born, you hope he will be a wolf, and fear he will be a worm. If a daughter, one hopes for a mouse and fears she will become a tiger.

Traditional

If the wife wishes to obtain her husband's affections, she must first obtain that of her in-laws.

Ban Zhao, Han Dynasty

Women and girls today are no longer interested in spinning and weaving; instead all they wish to do is go shopping.

Ge Hung, Han Dynasty

Bitter indeed it is to be born a woman.
It is difficult to imagine anything so low.

Fu Xuan (a man), Three Kingdoms Period

❀

A girl is reared without joy or love,
And no one in her family really cares for her.
Grown-up, she has to hide in the inner rooms,
Cover her head, be afraid to look others in the face.
And no one sheds a tear when she is married off,
All ties with her own kin are abruptly severed.

Fu Xuan, Three Kingdoms Period

❀

The clouds of my hair-locks are not yet dry,
The shining side tresses are raven-black.
From aside I stick a golden needle in it,
My hair finished, I smile and look round at my lover.

Zhao Luanluan, Tang Dynasty.

The tears on my pillow,
And the rain falling on the steps,
Separated only by the window pane,
They drip down all night long.

Xu Xueying, Tang Dyasty

The mountain road is steep,
The stone paths dangerous,
But it is not the road that pains me,
It is my love for you.

Yu Xuanzhi to her lover Li Yi, Tang Dynasty

Separated from you, what can I offer?
Only this poem, stained with bright tears.
Yu Xuanzhi to Li Yi, Tang Dynasty

❀

Bitterly I search for the right words,
Writing this poem under the silver lamp.
Yu Xuanzhi to Wen Tingyun, Tang Dynasty

❀

Because of the rain and clouds,
He lost his kingdom.
Sadly and forlorn,
A few willows stand before the hall,
In spring their leaves try in vain,
To compete with curved eyebrows*.
(* "woman" + "eyebrow" = "flirt")
Xue Tao, Tang Dynasty

Beauty both false and genuine beguiles man's heart
    alike,
But since the counterfeit appeals less than the true,
A fox posing as a woman will do a man but little
    harm,
Only for a day or so can she deceive his eyes.
But a woman bewitching like a fox, will do indeed
    great harm,
For days and months on end, she'll keep man's heart
    entranced.

Bo Juyi, Tang Dynasty

We knew the rain and clouds
In the intimacy of the curtained chamber,
Where our deep passion united us.
Now after the banquet, how empty is the room.
There is nothing to lose but myself,
In dreams of spring.

Li Yu, Five Dynasties and Ten Kingdoms

We meet south of the painted hall
One brief moment, shivering with fear.
Since I risk so much in coming here,
You must give me all your love.

Li Yu, Five Dynasties and Ten Kingdoms

Deep into the night I listen to the rain,
Dripping, dripping on the leaves
That he can't hear that sound again,
Is breaking my heart.

Li Chingzhao, Song Dynasty

❀

Between you and me there is far too much emotion,
And this causes our red-hot quarrels.

Lady Guan Daosheng to her husband Zhao Mengfu,
Yuan Dynasty

❀

Alive we'll sleep under the same quilt,
Dead we'll share the same coffin.

Lady Guan Daosheng to Zhao Mengfu, Yuan Dynasty

❀

In later life, all I want is peace and quiet.
Ten thousand matters are not my concern,

Wang Wei, Tang Dynasty

Cities and towns float on the bank.
The distant sky bobs on the waves.

Wang Wei goes boating, Tang Dynasty

The floating clouds always cover the sun
And I, I long for my home town of Chang-an

Li Bo, Tang Dynasty

Rolling up the scrolls of books,
Glee turns to madness.

Du Fu packs up to celebrate a victory, Tang Dynasty

Ten thousand miles this autumn,
I will always be a traveler.

Du Fu, Tang Dynasty

Bitter hardships and regrets mix and gray my temples.

Du Fu, Tang Dynasty

This feeling, must it wait to become memory?
The moment passes, and is already lost in fog.

Li Shangyin, Tang Dynasty

Last night's stars, last night's breeze,
West of the painted chamber, east of the cassia hall,
My body has no colorful phoenix wings.

Li Shangyin the morning after the night before,
Tang Dynasty

Meeting is hard. Separation harder.
The east wind fades, the flowers wilt.

Li Shangyin, Tang Dynasty

❀

Candles weep until they become ash.

Li Shangyin, Tang Dynasty

❀

Do the birds in the trees know their fate?
We share this moment, with only the sky between us.

Li Shangyin, Tang Dynasty

❀

The hut by the stream, silent and deserted,
Yet the hibiscus still blooms and falls

Wang Wei reminds us that life goes on,
Tang Dynasty

I sleep in spring, unconscious of the dawn,
When songs of birds were heard on every lawn;
At night came sounds of rain and wind that blew,
How many a blossom fell there no one knew.

Meng Haoran, Tang Dynasty

I think of you this autumn night,
As I stroll beneath the cool night air,
Pine cones fall on the empty mountain,
But the secluded man stays awake.

Wei Yingwu, Tang Dynasty

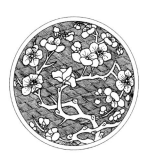

What man is not stirred by thoughts of his home?

Li Bo, Tang Dynasty

⁂

The lady is happy in her chamber,
Spring day, dressed up she climbs a tower of jade.
Suddenly she sees, in the fields a green willow,
And wishes she had not sent her husband away to
  seek fortune.

Wang Changling's noblewoman feels a little frisky,
Tang Dynasty

⁂

Green sea, blue sky, night after night her heart sinks.

Li Shangyin wonders how it must feel to be
trapped on the Moon and looking down upon
the Earth, Tang Dynasty

⁂

I sit and fret, and my red face grows old.

Li Bo, Tang Dynasty

Separated in death, and you are choked with sobbing,
Separated in life and grief strikes every day.

Du Fu, Tang Dynasty

❀

Without you, loneliness is my only companion.

Du Fu, Tang Dynasty

❀

In the deep night, I suddenly dreamed of the days of
my youth,
And woke in tears, my makeup running.

Bo Juyi records a female musician's lament,
Tang Dynasty

❀

Sunset over a high tower.
Inside, someone grieves.

Li Bo, Tang Dynasty

If someone knows where Spring goes,
Call Spring back to stay.

Huang Tingjian, Liao Dynasty

❀

Remembering things past,
Like a dream,
Tears drip darkly.

Zhou Bangyan, Liao Dynasty

❀

Many years of separation: Wrong! Wrong! Wrong!

Lu Yu, Kin Dynasty

❀

Take an emancipated woman in marriage, and you
will endure the might of the tigress.

Anon., Qing Dynasty

A good man and a virtuous wife are perfect harmony.

Traditional

❋

I can behead a general and destroy my enemies, rampage without fear, but if trapped amongst flowers*, I am indolent despite my power.
(*i.e. fall in love)

Anon., Qing Dynasty

❋

Tender passions are a tiger's cage.

Traditional

❋

Forgetting his white hair and wrinkles, the young women let the old man pay for their smiles.

Anon., Qing Dynasty

Liu Lang is not like a lily, a lily is like Liu Lang.

Yang Caisi turns on the charm, Tang Dynasty

✿

As the seasons turn, there is autumn in my heart

Lu Yun, Eastern Jin Dynasty

✿

A distant heart creates a wilderness around it.

Tao Qian, Eastern Jin Dynasty

✿

The flying birds two by two return. In these things there lies a deep meaning; yet when we would express it, words suddenly fail us.

Tao Qian, Eastern Jin Dynasty

Even yet, what was said when we left each other . . .
whenever I remember it, I weep to myself, of parting,
of distance.
Wang Huan, Southern and Northern Dynasties

The beauty waits, and waits, but no one comes.
Xie Tiao, Southern and Northern Dynasties

Once my carriage and horse goes east or west, she
won't think of this night again.
Xie Tiao, Southern and Northern Dynasties

Floating clouds have no place to rest.
Bao Quan, Southern and Northern Dynasties

✹

She almost laughs, but the laugh comes out as tears.
Shen Yue, Southern and Northern Dynasties

✹

If you abandon me, I will not complain. Men have always been this way.
Cui Yingying (attrib. Yuan Zhen), Tang Dynasty

✹

For whom shall I make up and adorn myself now?
Cui Yingying to her absent lover
(attrib. Yuan Zhen), Tang Dynasty

Heaven so reacts to a woman of exceptional beauty that she ruins either herself or those around her.

Yuan Zhen, Tang Dynasty

I have given up my joy and lost my beauty, and now toss and turn and keep to my bed. I don't care who sees me faded like this, save him alone who brought it to pass.

Cui Yingying (attrib. Yuan Zhen), Tang Dynasty

We must give the love we had for each other, to the person whom Fate has given us.

Cui Yingying, (attrib. Yuan Zhen), Tang Dynasty

When lovers are agreed, not even their parents can control them.

Bai Xingqian, Tang Dynasty

At fifteen I stopped scowling. I desired my dust to be mingled with yours. Forever and forever and forever.

The River-Merchant's Wife (attrib. Li Bo),
Tang Dynasty

Night and day are given over to pleasure,
And they think it will last for a thousand autumns.

Li Bo, Tang Dynasty

All that time, you've been thinking of home.
And all that time, my heart breaking.

Li Bo, Tang Dynasty

If we are human, alive, have feelings,
tears must wet our breast.

Du Fu, Tang Dynasty

Herself loving, she's quick to take out the mirror.

Liang Huang, Tang Dynasty

You ask when I'll be home.
So far, there's no "when."

Li Shangyin, Tang Dynasty

Don't say: "Parting tastes like pain."

Wen Tingyun, Tang Dynasty

❦

Half shy she is half joyful.

Wei Zhuang, Tang Dynasty

❦

Waking I knew a dream, and the sadness like a pouring flood.

Wei Zhuang, Tang Dynasty

❦

How long ago we said goodbye, our tears mingling together.

Li Cunxu, Five Dynasties and Ten Kingdoms

I knew my mind, I guessed your heart, but love must answer Heaven.

Li Yu, Five Dynasties and Ten Kingdoms

❀

I wonder where sorrow comes from?

Su Shi, Song Dynasty

❀

Once departed, when will I see her again?
My sleeves and lapels are still stained with her tears.

Chin Guan, Song Dynasty

❀

During his lifetime, an individual should devote his efforts to create happiness and to enjoy it, and also to keep it in store in society so that individuals of the future may also enjoy it, one generation doing the same for the next and so on unto infinity.

Chen Duxiu, Republican Period

The beauties of the Han Dynasty and Tang Dynasty
end in common dust.

Xin Chizhi, Kin Dynasty

※

Listless with Spring, she combs again already-
ordered hair.

Li Chingzhao, Song Dynasty

※

Geese fly over, cut my heart
Them too I used to know*
  (*Geese are a symbol of letters and communication)

Li Chingzhao, Song Dynasty

I'm sure that if a young girl sighs thus, there must be sorrow in her heart.

Wang Shifu, Yuan Dynasty

✻

Behind my maidenly screen are solitude and silence.
There is no way for me to enjoy the fragrant Spring.

Cui Yingying (attrib. Wang Shifu), Yuan Dynasty

✻

Now after your stay with me this night,
I worship and adore you.

Chang to Cui Yingying (attrib. Wang Shifu),
Yuan Dynasty

✻

The waters of the golden pool are covered with sleeping mandarin ducks. The wind has blown open the embroidered curtain. The parrot has noticed it.

Hung Niang realizes that the lovers have been found out,
attrib. Wang Shifu, Yuan Dynasty

The spirit of spring is loving, of autumn, stern, of summer joyous, and of winter, sad.

Dong Zhongshu, Han Dynasty

❀

Beauty runs a pawnshop, accepting only the hearts of men.

Zhu Xiang, Republican Period

❀

Do you not see, master, the hibiscus?
Its beauty seldom lasts a day.

Bao Zhao, Southern and Northern Dynasties

❀

A man has only one death.

Sima Qian, Han Dynasty

There is no greater happppiness than freedom from worry, and there is no greater wealth than contentment.

Lao Zi, Spring and Autumn Period

I sing a sad song, instead of weeping
Stare into the distance, instead of returning
Thinking of my homeland, so many memories
I want to go back, but no one is home
I want to cross the river, but there is no boat
I cannot utter the thoughts in my heart
My belly churns like grinding wheels

Yue-fu: Nineteen Ancient Poems, Han Dynasty

He who can read his fair lady's thoughts,
Only he is without peer in the arena of love.

Anon., Ming Dynasty

卍

A man thinks he knows, but a woman knows better.

Traditional

卍

The Hwai's blue stream may quickly pass my door,
But thou must longer stay I now implore;
The shining moon will light thy journey home,
Deep floods of spring each eve to me will come.

Wang Changling, Tang Dynasty

These borders wild no birds or blossoms cheer,
And late the year when signs of spring appear.
Our Princess, angel-like will there descend,
To tardy spring her maiden beauty lend.

Sun Di consoles a woman married to barbarians,
Tang Dynasty

❀

Thy spotless beauty puts to shame the snow.

Qiu Wei, Tang Dynasty

❀

To worthier hands I leave the rule of state,
To enjoy my wine and while my time away.

Li Shizhi, Tang Dynasty

❀

My heart is trembling like a falling leaf,
As autumn's voice I hear with bitter grief.

Su Ting, Tang Dynasty

When all is red and purple, spring is surely due.
Zhu Xi is supposed to be talking about flowers . . .
Tang Dynasty

✿

The signs of early spring attract the poet's eye,
Ere willows' tender yellow turns to greenish dye.
Nor will he wait till tender shrubs in splendor blow,
For then the crowd can also note the floral show.
Yang Quyuan likes them young. Flowers, that is.
Tang Dynasty

✿

The spring is cold, though perfumed roses lull my
    dream,
Enclosed in bowers, an idle swallow I but seem.
Zheng Gu misses her husband, Tang Dynasty

Spring colors cannot be kept within your garden.
Ye Shi warns against over-possessiveness, Song Dynasty

※

Where fallen flowers engrossed my thoughts I there
   too long had stayed,
For searching fragrant herbs my coming home was
   much delayed.

Wang Anshi, Song Dynasty

※

Before the springtime showers only buds were seen,
When time for showers ended naught but leafy green.
Across the next wall bees and butterflies have flown,
Believing charms of spring the neighboring gardens
own.

Wang Jia seeks naughty pastures new, Tang Dynasty

The flowers know that soon must haste the end of
   spring,
So each in varied beauty or in sweetness vies.

Han Yu, Tang Dynasty

❀

If we do not enjoy ourselves today,
The days and months will pass us by.

Book of Songs, Zhou Dynasty

❀

Man's life should be spent in joy;
Why wait in vain for wealth and honor?

Yang-yun to Sun Huicong, Han Dynasty

❀

Inscribe on your heart every inch of the time at
sunset.

Ruan Zhi wants to seize the day, Han Dynasty

Where shall we bind our hearts as one?
Xiao Su, Southern and Northern Dynasties

Do not too quickly tell her of my will:
Too sudden favors might upset her so
Her broken notes would startle nesting birds
And frighten crows atop the palace trees.
Ma Zhiyuan writes of a delicately-dispositioned lady,
Yuan Dynasty

Parting brought twin lines of tears.
Gu Dadian, Ming Dynasty

Don't think about the sorrows of the world;
You will only make yourself feel wretched.
Book of Songs, Spring and Autumn Period

Life is but a dream.

Li Bo, Tang Dynasty

Even the Goddess of Mercy sheds tears.

Traditional

In the forest, Spring flowers blooming
Spring birds singing, life is blest
Strong spring breeze is swiftly zooming
Through the trees and up my dress.

Yue-fu: Zi Ye Songs, Southern and Northern Dynasties

Sources

漂

[Various] (1992) *Chinese-English Bilingual Series of Chinese Classics: Han'ei Duizhao Zhongguo Gudian Mingzhu Congshu.* (10 vols) Changsha: Hunan Publishing House. Birch, C. (1965) *Anthology of Chinese Literature: From early times to the fourteenth century.* New York: Grove Press. Chen, S. (1981) *Chengyu Cidian: Chinese Idioms and Their English Equivalents.* Taibei: Southern Materials Center. de Bary, W. et al. (1963) *Sources of Chinese Tradition.* New York: Columbia University Press. Giles, H. (1916) *Strange Tales from a Chinese Studio.* Shanghai: Kelly and Walsh. Hom, M. (1987) *Songs of Gold Mountain: Cantonese Rhymes from San Francisco Chinatown.* Berkeley: University of California Press. Lockhart, J. (1903) *A Manual of Chinese Quotations: Being a translation of the Ch'eng Yu K'ao.* Hong Kong: Kelly and Walsh. Mao, Z. (1972) *Six Essays on Military Affairs.* Beijing: Foreign Languages Press. McNaughton, W. (1974). *Chinese Literature: An Anthology from the Earliest Times to the Present Day.* Rutland, VT: Charles Tuttle. Tan, S. (1997) *Zhongguo Chengyu Xuancui: Best Chinese Idioms.* (2 vols) Hong Kong: Hai Feng Publishing. Ts'ai, T. (1932) *Chinese Poems in English Rhyme.* New York: Greenwood Press. van Gulik, R. (1974) *Sexual Life in Ancient China.* Leiden: E.J. Brill. Yip, W. (1976) *Chinese Poetry: Major Modes and Genres.* Berkeley: University of California Press.